Published by Four Bites.

FourBites.net is your source for restaurant and cooking intelligence in Buffalo, from award-winning investigative reporter and restaurant critic Andrew Galarneau.

ISBN: 978-1-970895-00-1

I was 16 when I headed to the University at Buffalo, determined to become a book author. At 17, I helped launch Generation, a weekly feature magazine by and for students. It turned out that writing about the real world was more interesting than making things up.

I was a reporter for the Concord (N.H.) Monitor, St. Petersburg Times, and Lowell Sun before my hometown newspaper The Buffalo News hired me in 1997. I was a prizewinning investigative reporter, food editor, and restaurant critic for the News before leaving in 2023 to launch Four Bites, my digital food report.

I am 58 now, with a million published words, but I finally got to write a book. Thanks to Hannah Gordon of Gordon Publishing Collective, I was able to distill a decade of daily reporting on Buffalo foodways into a compact toolkit for better eating in Buffalo.

As ever, please send suggestions and corrections to me at andrew@fourbites.net, so the 2027 edition can be even better. And thanks for reading – because everybody's gotta eat.

Introduction

Where to Eat in Buffalo 2026 collects my best tips on eating better in Buffalo and Western New York.

That's my byline on the cover. But the truth is more complicated.

The Four Bites report is a community effort. Since 2012, when I started writing about food in Buffalo, I have implored everyone who would listen to drop a dime on tasty news.

Today, about 100 people send me texts, emails, or photos about things they notice. A dish, a sign that says RESTAURANT COMING. Some contributors will park their car at a new restaurant, go inside, and emerge with a photo of the menu and the cellphone number of the owner.

Some I have never met in person. Others have become regular dinner guests. Because my Tipsters Get Fed policy stipulates that a tip I need to check out in person equals an invite to dinner on me. So there is a built-in incentive to hit me with the new hotness.

That's how I find half of the truly hidden gems. Its breadth and depth are due to its unsung heroes. This, my first book, is dedicated to them. Thank you, you know who you are.

As for-profit news companies wither, community-based news sources will become even more important. Communities need reliable information just like they need reliable water and stoplights.

Towards that end, I helped found The Buffalo Hive, a 501(c)(3) nonprofit whose website—thebuffalohive.com—aims to become the community calendar Buffalo deserves. A digital town square where you can easily answer questions like "What live music can I enjoy Thursday night?"

Buffalo deserves it. We're working on it. 501(c)(3) means it's tax deductible, by the way, if you want to support this endeavor, led by Fredonia journalism professor and former Buffalo News colleague Elmer Ploetz.

We're all trying to make Buffalo better. Thank you for your support.

Andrew Galarneau

P.S.: As a professional fact checker, I know that as soon as this book is printed, some details will be overtaken by events. To avoid disappointment, call the restaurant before you make plans, or at least review its recent social media.

Index of Deliciousness

1 99 Fast Food
2 Abyssinia Ethiopian Cuisine
3 Alibaba Kebab
4 Almandi
5 Almaza Grill
6 Amabel Provisions
7 Anastasia's Artisan Bread Bakery
8 As-Salam Diner and Kabab House
9 Asia Food Mart
10 Bailey Seafood
11 Bamboo Ridge
12 Bandana's Bar and Grille
13 Bar-Bill Tavern
14 Barrel + Brine
15 Beacon Grille
16 Bflo Pizza Bistro
17 Billy Club
18 Bistro 93
19 Bistro Avera
20 Bloom & Rose Deli
21 Bocce on Bailey
22 BreadHive
23 Britesmith Brewing
24 Buffalo Fresh
25 Buffalo Tikka House
26 Butter Block Bakery and Patisserie
27 Cafe 59
28 Caffe @ Amy's
29 Carmelo's Coat of Arms
30 Casa Azul
31 China Taste
32 City Fare Cafe
33 Clay Handi
34 Coco Bar & Bistro
35 Colombo Spice
36 Connor's
37 Cozy Thai
38 Crave King
39 D'Alfonso's Italian Imports
40 The Dapper Goose
41 Dick & Jenny's
42 DiTondo
43 Dog & Pony Saloon
44 The Dove
45 Duff's Sheridan Patio
46 Dulce Hogar Bakery
47 Eagle House

48 El Encanto
49 Extra Extra Pizza
50 Fairbanks
51 Falafel Bar
52 Falafel House Bakery and Grill
53 Family Thai
54 Farm Shop
55 Farmers & Artisans
56 The Fire Spot
57 Five Points Bakery
58 Forno Napoli
59 Fortuna's
60 Frank Gourmet Hot Dogs
61 Gene McCarthy's Old First Ward Brewing Co.
62 Giancarlo's Sicilian Steakhouse
63 Glen Park Tavern
64 Golden Hill Asian Cuisine
65 Gondola Macaroni Products
66 Grange Community Kitchen
67 Graylynn
68 Gypsy Parlor
69 Hayes Seafood House
70 Hilltop Restaurant
71 Holy Feast
72 Home Taste
73 Hot Mama's Canteen
74 House of Sandwich
75 Hydraulic Hearth
76 Imperial Pizza
77 Inchin's Bamboo Garden
78 Ilio DiPaolo's Restaurant
79 Inizio
80 International House
81 Iron Tail Tavern
82 Jasmine Thai
83 Jay's Artisan Pizzeria
84 K Dara Noodle Bar
85 Kith & Kin Bakeshop & Bistro
86 Konbini
87 Kostas Family Restaurant
88 Kuni's
89 La Casa de Sabores
90 La Divina Tacos
91 La Flor Bakery
92 La Oaxaqueña Taqueria
93 Lexington Co-op
94 Lin Asian Market
95 Little Lamb Hot Pot

96 Lloyd Taco Factory
97 Louie's Deli & Imports
98 Louisiana Cookery
99 Lovejoy Pizzeria
100 Lucky Day Whiskey Bar
101 Mahar Moe
102 Maizal Mexican Kitchen & Mezcaleria
103 Manito Taco Shop
104 Marble + Rye
105 Mayback's Deli
106 Miller's Thumb Bakery & Cafe
107 Mira
108 Mojo Market
109 Monte's Grocery Deli
110 Moriarty Meats and Cafe Bar Moriarty
111 Mulberry Italian Ristorante
112 Nana Peruvian Kitchen
113 Natalie's Mediterranean Eatery
114 Nellai Banana Leaf
115 Nephew's BBQ
116 Niagara Cafe
117 Nine & Night Thai Cuisine
118 OG Dumpling House
119 Olisi's NY Pizza
120 Oralia
121 Pattaya Street Food
122 Parker's Great British Institution
123 Peking Quick One
124 Pham's Kitchen
125 Pho Dollar
126 Picasso's Pizza
127 Pinoy Boi
128 Pita Gourmet
129 Pizzeria Florian
130 Prescott's Provisions
131 Public Espresso
132 Quenelle
133 Raha Coffee Shop
134 Remedy House
135 Risa's Deli & Catering
136 Rizzo's House of Parm
137 Royal Family Restaurant
138 Sato Ramen
139 Savage Wheat Project
140 Sahar Bakery
141 Sevens

142 Savor
143 Schwabl's
144 Shamus
145 Shawarma House
146 Shibam Mediterranean Restaurant
147 Simply Soul
148 Sofra Restaurant and Bakery
149 Sophia's
150 Southern Belle Diner
151 Southern Junction
152 Spresh
153 Strong Hearts Buffalo
154 Suenos de Azucar Bakery
155 That Greek Guy Bakery
156 Taqueria Los Mayas
157 Thai House
158 This Little Pig
159 Tienda Monte Alban
160 Tiny Thai
161 Tortuga
162 Ukrainian-American Civic Center
163 Undergrounds Coffee
164 Vinnie's Minis

165 Wasabi Amherst
166 Waxlight Bar a Vin
167 Wayland Brewing Company
168 West Rose
169 Wiechec's Lounge
170 Winfield's Pub
171 Wok & Roll
172 Woo Chon Korea House
173 Yalley's African Restaurant
174 Yankee BBQ
175 Yemen Star
176 Zambistro
177 Zereshk

99 FAST FOOD

3398 Bailey Ave., 99fastfood.com, 716-836-6058
Hours: 10:30 a.m.-9 p.m. Monday-Saturday,
10:30 a.m.-8 p.m. Sunday.

Buffalo's Vietnamese veteran scores with reliable
pho and bun noodle salad bowls, grilled pork on
rice, a hefty pad thai, and the best fried pork-mush-
room-noodle stuffed rolls ("Vietnamese egg rolls")
ever. Spicy curry stir-fry and teriyaki chicken plates
are also justly popular.

ABYSSINIA ETHIOPIAN CUISINE

617 Main St., abyssinia-ethiopian.square.site,
716-563-6602
Hours: 10:30 a.m.-8:30 p.m. Tuesday-Saturday. Closed
Sunday, Monday.

Get your kik alitcha and doro wot fix at Buffalo's
only Ethiopian restaurant. Zelalem Gemmeda
has served Buffalo since 2011. Vegan and carni-
vore-pleasing dishes arrayed on flapjack-like injera
bread are the stars here, along
with crispy beef sambusas
in thin-skinned pastry.

ALIBABA KEBAB

900 William St., 716-800-2222
Hours: 11 a.m.-midnight Monday-Saturday. Closed Sunday.

827 Military Road, Kenmore, 716-919-1111
Hours: 11 a.m.-midnight daily.

1100 Southwestern Blvd., West Seneca, 716-608-3333
Hours: 11 a.m.-midnight daily.

All locations share the same webiste: alibaba-kebab.com.

Kebab wraps in fresh-made bread, and rice boxes sporting your choice of protein over basmati pilaf, lavished with garlic mayonnaise, lead the board. Alibaba's tandoori wings, marinated in spiced yogurt then fired to a crisp in the tandoor's blast-furnace heat, are another great Buffalo wing.

ALMANDI

797 Broadway, 716-853-1090
Hours: 10 a.m.-10 p.m. daily.

Yemeni family
restaurant offers
grilled chick-
en and fish, and
lamb haneeth,
oven-braised to lush-
ness, traditionally eaten by the handful on a platter of
rice. Saltah and fahsah stews arrive bubbling, topped
with fenugreek foam, best eaten with fresh bread.
Enjoy complimentary broth, a traditional welcoming
gesture, and "red tea," made of black tea, cardamom,
and lots of sugar.

ALMAZA GRILL

9370 Transit Road, East Amherst, almazagrill.com, 716-276-8080
Hours: noon-9 p.m. daily.

Peruvian-marinated rotisserie chicken with garlic mayonnaise and zippy herb sauce is a main draw, takeout or dine-in. Then there's the Lebanese side, with kofta, kibbe, and loubie bzeit, green beans braised with garlic and tomato. Check out the cake case for dessert ideas.

AMABEL PROVISIONS

1006 Elmwood Ave., amabelprovisions.com, 716-277-6823
Hours: 11 a.m.-6 p.m. Thursday, Friday,
10 a.m.-5 p.m. Saturday, 11 a.m.-3 p.m. Sunday. Closed
Monday-Wednesday.

Buffalo has a proper cheese shop again, curating
notable cheeses available by the piece, board, or
assortment. Sandwiches are assembled to order, and
the cheesemonger can help you find your happy place,
curdwise. Chocolate, preserves, pretzels, and more
fill the shelves. A wine bar is expected to join it this
season, as of press time.

Anastasia's Artisan Bread Bakery

236 Zimmerman St., North Tonawanda, anastasiasbread.com,
716-906-4135
Hours: 8 a.m.-1 p.m. Wednesday-Monday. Closed Tuesday.

Dark rye beloved by northern Europeans, cardamom knots, baguettes, financiers, and much more comes out fresh every morning in North Tonawanda. A couple of Russian engineers with a home-based baking enterprise went brick-and-mortar in November.

As-Salam Diner and Kabab House

1389 Bailey Ave., assalamkababhouse.com, 716-725-0603
Hours: 11 a.m.-9 p.m. Monday,
11 a.m.-10 p.m. Tuesday-Thursday, 5 p.m.-10 p.m. Friday,
11 a.m.-10 p.m. Saturday, Sunday.

Cheery servers at Bangladeshi family restaurant bear platters of sizzling lamb shashlik, vats of curry, and six types of made-to-order bread. Appetizers worth meeting include sauteed shrimp tucked into puffy puri bread, and a smashed potato samosa pastry with tamarind and yogurt sauces.

Asia Food Market

2055 Niagara Falls Blvd., Amherst, 716-691-0888
Hours: 9 a.m.-8 p.m. daily.

Biggest international grocery in Western New York, with fresh vegetables, live seafood market, meat, barbecue counter, plus extensive frozen goods. One-stop shopping for Chinese, Korean, Indian, Thai, Vietnamese, and other Asian cuisines.

BAILEY SEAFOOD

3316 Bailey Ave., baileyseafood.com, 716-833-1973
Hours: 3 p.m.-7 p.m. Tuesday-Thursday, noon-8 p.m. Friday,
3 p.m.-7 p.m. Saturday. Closed Sunday, Monday.

Takeout restaurant started as a seafood market in
1985 has built a dedicated following for fried fish
and shrimp, and more recently, seafood boils. Fried
haddock dinners and sandwiches, fried perch, and
seafood pastas are standouts.

BAMBOO RIDGE

244 Allen St., bambooridgethai.com, 716-235-8951
Hours: 11 a.m.-10 p.m. Monday-Thursday,
11 a.m.-midnight Friday, Saturday, noon-10 p.m. Sunday.

Burmese restaurateur Hla Thu brought his Thai, Burmese, Malaysian, and Chinese playbook to Allentown in November. Thai beef salad, Burmese biryani, coconut curries, and crispy whole fish are among popular offerings.

BANDANA'S
BAR AND GRILLE

930 Lake Road, Youngstown, bandanasbarandgrill.
com, 716-745-1010
Hours: 11 a.m.-10 p.m. Monday-Saturday,
noon-10 p.m. Sunday.

Adventurous scratch cooking within a holler of the
Lake Ontario shore, disguised as a scruffy biker
bar. Specials like char siu pork belly burnt ends
abound. Fried seafood Fridays and Mexican Sun-
days replete with
chimichangas, enchi-
ladas, and burritos
are a fixture.

Bar-Bill Tavern

185 Main St., East Aurora, barbill.com, 716-652-7959
Hours: 11:30 a.m.- 1 a.m. daily.

Wing and beef-on-weck landmark known for consistency and respectful wing presentation. So popular that regulars know to show up before doors open to get a lunchtime seat. Bar-Bill also offers the third leg of the Buffalo cuisine triad, with bar pizzas. Try the honey butter BBQ.

Barrel + Brine

155 Chandler St. Suite 3, barrelnbrine.com, 716-322-5756
Hours: noon-6 p.m. Friday, Saturday, noon-4 p.m.
Sunday. Closed Monday-Thursday.

Gobsmacking sandwiches and a full bar are notable offshoots of a fermentation-focused business hidden in a post-industrial building in Black Rock. Homegrown provider of a broad array of pickled vegetables, sauerkraut, and kombucha has so much more to offer than a pickle on a stick.

BEACON GRILLE

185 Allen St., beacongrille716.com, 716-413-3630
Hours: 4 p.m.-midnight Tuesday-Thursday, 4 p.m.-2
a.m. Friday, Saturday. Closed Sunday, Monday.

First-class dining from skilled veterans driving a
purpose-built, fire-centered kitchen. Local produce
and meat handled with care, touched by fire in subtle
and transformative ways. Capable servers, advanced
cocktail program, and housemade charcuterie make
for a topflight experience.

BFLO PIZZA BISTRO

388 Porter Ave.,
bflopizzabistro.com,
716-248-2240
Hours: 4 p.m.-8 p.m.
Wednesday, Thursday,
1 p.m.-8 p.m. Friday, Saturday.
Closed Sunday-Tuesday.

Lower West Side pizzeria born as a pandemic project has found its audience between D'Youville and Symphony Circle. Detroit-style pizza and spiffy salads are the heart of the menu. Especially recommended: vodka sauce pie with pesto, pepperoni with hot chile honey, and lemon pecorino salad.

BILLY CLUB

*9228 Allen St., billyclubbuffa-
lo.com, 716-331-3047*
Kitchen hours: 5 p.m.-10
p.m. Monday-Saturday,
10 a.m.-3 p.m. Sunday.
Closed Tuesday.
Bar hours: until 1 a.m. Monday, Wednesday, Thursday, 2
a.m. Friday, Saturday.

Chill supper club offers
lowkey dining sophisti-
cation and bar seats with
elevated view of Allentown
scene. Oysters, octopus,
and housemade pasta are
standards, along with the
Plato Dale cheeseburger.

BISTRO 93

15 Cedar St., Akron, 716-442-5363
Hours: 11 a.m.-10 p.m. Wednesday-Saturday,
11 a.m.-8 p.m. Sunday. Closed Monday, Tuesday.

It might seem weird to head to Akron for a taste of the tropics, but Bistro 93 is a breath of fresh air.. Oasis of cheer and tropically-inflected cooking driven by husband-and-wife team of restaurant veterans with a sense of humor. Duck wontons a la orange, fish in Caribbean outfits, and pastas aplenty are guaranteed.

BISTRO AVERA

555 Center St., Lewiston, facebook.com/bistroavera,
716-246-2035
Hours: 5 p.m.-9 p.m. Wednesday-Saturday.
Closed Sunday-Tuesday.

Stephen Pusateri brings decades of dedication to a
menu of playful originals executed with fine-dining
precision in cozy, unpretentious surroundings. Artful
touches abound throughout appetizers and entrees,
housemade breads and desserts.

BLOOM & ROSE DELI

27 Chandler St., Room 204a, thebloomandrose.com,
716-406-7522
Hours: 11 a.m.-4 p.m. Tuesday-Friday.
Closed Saturday-Monday. 365 Main St., Williamsville,
summer 2025

Samosa knishes are one of the ways this outfit takes
Jewish cuisine on trips to fascinating places. Expect
opening in former Monro Muffler location, with
beer and wine bar,
deli sandwiches, salads,
soups and Bloom &
Rose's lineup of knish-
es, and its beguiling
smoked egg salad.

Bocce on Bailey

4174 Bailey Ave., Amherst, bocceclubpizza.com,
716-833-1344
Hours: 10 a.m.-9 p.m. Sunday-Wednesday, 10 a.m.-10
p.m. Thursday, 10 a.m.-11 p.m. Friday, Saturday.

My childhood pizza favorite still works for me,
among the various Bocce-branded outlets else-
where. Cheese and pep "well done no trim," thank
you very much. Walking in from the February
frostbite to stand under
the oven-powered line
warmer always feels
like coming home.

BreadHive

402 Connecticut St., breadhive.com, 716-980-5623
Hours: 11 a.m.-2 p.m. daily

Worker-owned bakery and Elmwood-Bidwell Farmers Market fixture has a decade's experience crafting loaves of signature West Side Sourdough, bagels, and pretzels. Some are turned into sandwiches at its cafe, named after women superstars, with animal-involved and vegan versions. While you're there grab cookies, scones, muffins, granola, or something from the cooler of local products.

BRITESMITH BREWING

5611 Main St., Williamsville, britesmithbrewing.com, 716-650-4080

Hours: 4 p.m.-10 p.m. Monday-Thursday, 11 a.m.-11 p.m. Friday, Saturday, 11 a.m.-9 p.m. Sunday.

Brewpub with adventurous menu perched on the bank of Tonawanda Creek. Neapolitan pizzas range from pristine margherita to cheddar-bacon-ranch to The Lobstah, featuring Maine lobster on garlic cream. Korean cheesesteak with bulgogi and kimchi stand out among the usual sandwich suspects.

BUFFALO FRESH

284 Ontario St., buffalofreshmarkets.com, 716-582-0510
Hours: 9 a.m.-8 p.m. daily.

International grocery and bakery produces Iraqi sa-
moon loaves and cheese-topped manakeesh daily. In
the back, a steam table of fish, meat, rice, and vegetable choices awaits customers. In between is a world of
Arab and Persian groceries, well-stocked freezers, and
a halal meat counter. Sister store, without bakery, at
1018 Broadway across from Broadway Market.

Buffalo Tikka House

948 Main St., 716-240-9324
Hours: 10:30 a.m.-10 p.m. Saturday-Thursday,
10:30 a.m.- 1 p.m., 4 p.m.-10 p.m.

Full-force Bangladeshi Indian restaurant across the street from the Buffalo Medical Campus is an oasis of fragrant curries and fresh-made bread. Notable dishes include paneer tikka, chicken achari, and garlic chili lamb. My favorite Indian restaurant in the City of Buffalo.

BUTTER BLOCK
BAKERY AND PATISSERIE

426 Rhode Island St., butterblockshop.com, 716-424-0027
Hours: 8 a.m.-2 p.m. Wednesday, 8 a.m.-noon Thursday,
8 a.m.-2 p.m. Friday-Sunday. Closed Monday, Tuesday.

Paris-level croissants and wildcards like pretzel
croissants draw daily pilgrims to Five Points. Holiday
lines suggest the pies, quiches, and cakes from Col-
leen Stillwell's crew are worth the wait.Look for the
seasonal danishes, but buy anything you can get your
hands on, honestly.

CAFE 59

62 Allen St., cafe59.com, 716-883-1880
Hours: 11 a.m.-10 p.m. daily.

Allentown's essential restaurant helps denizens get their daily bread, often in striking fashion. Hand-dipped chicken tenders make my favorite chicken finger sub, but there's always something for everyone, including polenta "wings" and a vegan soup du jour.

CAFFE @ AMY'S

3234 Main St., 716-832-6666
Hours: 7 a.m.-8:30 p.m.
Monday-Saturday,
7 a.m.-4:30 p.m. Sunday.

Cafe Aroma operators took over the University Heights veteran Amy's Place, keeping Amy's standards like lentilberry wraps while adding Aroma touches. Veggie "wet shoes," lentil chili over curly-Q fries, is still one of the vegan stoner classics available, plus a full coffee bar.

CARMELO'S COAT OF ARMS

425 Center St., Lewiston, carmeloslewiston.com,716-754-2311
Hours: 5 p.m.-8:30 p.m. Wednesday, Thursday, 5 p.m.-9 p.m. Friday, Saturday. Closed Sunday-Tuesday.

Carmelo Raimondi took over his father's restaurant and set his own standard of excellence with focused dishes drawing on local ingredients and evocative Italian and Asian-influenced compositions. Don't miss the crispy calamari salad with smoked peanuts and chile-lime vinaigrette.

Casa Azul

191 Allen St., casaazulbuffalo.com, 716-331-3869
Hours: 4 p.m.-11 p.m. Monday-Thursday,
4 p.m.-2 a.m. Friday, Saturday. Closed Sunday.

Housemade tortillas, housemade salsas, fresh-squeezed margaritas, and the city's best chicken taco draw crowds to Allen and Elmwood. Mole verde enchiladas, cod in corn-poblano chowder, and oxtail taquitos are fine Mexican dining in the heart of Allentown. Note: Casa Azul also sells its tortillas.

CHINA TASTE

1280 Sweet Home Road, chinatastebuffalo.com,
716-568-0080
Hours: 10:30 a.m.-9:30 p.m. Monday-Wednesday,
Friday, Saturday, 10:30 a.m.-9 p.m. Sunday.
Closed Thursday.

First-rate Chinese from a highly trained chef makes
lacy dumplings and sweet-and-sour pork must-or-
ders. With complimentary peanuts and kimchi, atten-
tive servers, and a speedy kitchen, this is a well-run
outfit. Cold Korean noodles, sea cucumber, and West
Lake beef soup beckon.

CITY FARE CAFE

438 Main St., 716-907-5600
Hours: 11 a.m.-2 p.m. Monday-Friday.
Closed Saturday, Sunday.

City Fare has the soup-salad-sandwich thing figured out. From vegan to carnivore, lowkey to spicy, City Fare has a sandwich for you. The Malibu Barbie offers turkey, bacon, avocado spread, tomato and lettuce. Little Nicky is pork, fennel, rapini, garlic, and provolone on a Luigi's roll. There's usually three soups of the day, worth considering.

CLAY HANDI

3054 Delaware Ave., Kenmore, clayhandibuffalony.com, 716-877-7797
Hours: 9 a.m.-2 a.m. daily.

Pakistani kebabs, curries, and braises, all served in clay vessels. In fact, everything is - order a jug of mango lassi for the table and everyone gets clay cups. Haleem, a savory mash of lentils, grain, and meat, comes in lamb, chicken, or beef. Vegan triumphs include deeply caramelized bhindi (okra) masala, and smoky eggplant baingan bharta. Under construction at publication, the new restaurant is expected to open in the spring.

Coco Bar & Bistro

888 Main St., cocobuffalo.com, 716-885-1885
Hours: 11:30 a.m.-10 p.m. Monday-Thursday, 11:30 a.m.-11 p.m. Friday, 4 p.m.-11 p.m. Saturday, 4 p.m.-9 p.m. Sunday.

One of the finest restaurants within walking distance of the Theater District offers a rare-for-Buffalo glimpse of French-inspired cuisine. Frites with mussels and Puy lentil salad with beets, carrots, and chevre are notable starters. Steak frites, trout du jour, coq a vin, and lamb bolognese are standard-bearers.

COLOMBO SPICE

265 Kenmore Ave., Tonawanda, colombo-spice.res-menu.com, 716-810-1282

Hours: 11 a.m.-9:30 p.m. Tuesday-Thursday, 11 a.m.-10 p.m. Friday, Saturday, 11 a.m.-9 p.m. Sunday.

Sri Lankan cooks now dispense life-sustaining meals where Jagat Seth and his brother Jai Raj once reigned as kings of the $.99 breakfast with a side of sass. Besides terrific lentil doughnuts, the dish that's really caught my attention is the special dolphin kothu. Cheese, chicken, bread, and a weapons-grade level of chile heat all in one irresistible package for those who dare.

CONNOR'S

3465 Seneca St., West Seneca, connorswestseneca.com,
716-674-9945
Hours: noon-9 p.m. Monday-Saturday. Closed Sunday.

Family restaurant does brisk business in wings, fried
calamari, and fish fries, but has more to offer. Like
Detroit-style pizza, steamed clams, liver and onions
with bacon, and pastas like the estimable french onion soup chicken.

CozyThai

39 Evans St., Hamburg, cozythaihamburg.com, 716-648-1016
Hours: 11:30 a.m. to 9:30 p.m. Monday-Saturday,
4 to 9:30 p.m. Sunday.

Family-run restaurant updated after the pandemic
with a sleek dining room. Classic curries and salads
hit the spot, including whole fried fish. But consider
pho, Vietnamese beef noodle soup, and seafood and
ramen noodles with tea
leaf sauce, inspired by the
cooks' heritages.

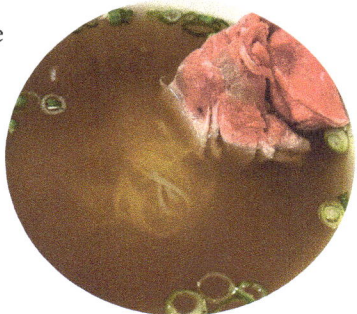

CRAVE KING

2693 South Park Ave., Lackawanna, 716-783-9743
Hours: 11 a.m.-9 p.m. Wednesday-Monday,
9 a.m.-6 p.m. Tuesday.

Fresh bread and vegetable stew stirs the soul at
this lowkey Yemeni restaurant. There might be one
cook on duty, but you will have his full attention.
Ful medames, grilled kebabs, and chicken galla-
ba, sauteed chicken breast on hummus, are also
standouts.

D'ALFONSO'S
ITALIAN IMPORTS

162 Allen St
Hours: 10 a.m.-5 p.m. Tuesday-Satuday.
Closed Sunday, Monday.

Sandwiches on puccia rolls made from Italian cheeses and charcuterie are a main draw at Jeffrey Dalfonso's Italianate sandwich shop and grocery. Pick up fresh buffalo-milk mozzarella, get a proper espresso with bubbly water chaser, or a quart of Dalfonso's meatballs in sauce.

THE DAPPER GOOSE

491 Amherst St., thedapper-goose.com, 716-551-0716
Hours: 5 p.m-9 p.m.
Wednesday-Saturday,
5 p.m.-8 p.m. Sunday.
Closed Monday, Tuesday.

Casually cool dining spot with well-honed dishes small and large that change with the seasons. Get the fried cauliflower with Green Goddess dressing, the blackened green beans with pepitas and charred onion aioli, then decide on the rest. Cocktails start with the parsley-and-celery-forward Broken Garden Tools.

Dick & Jenny's

1270 Baseline Road, Grand Island, dickandjennysny.com, 716-775-5047
Hours: 5 p.m.-9 p.m. Tuesday-Saturday.
Closed Sunday, Monday.

Buffalo's best Cajun-Creole restaurant is run by New Orleans restaurant lifers transplanted to Grand Island by Hurricane Katrina. Fat shrimp nestled into Colby cheese corn grits, blackened catfish, and properly inky gumbo nails the authenticity test. From the never-ending basket of cornbread and scones to Thursdays featuring a teen piano phenom, Dick and Jenny Benz make it nice.

DiTondo

370 Seneca St., ditondo1904.com
Hours: 5 p.m.-9 p.m. Wednesday-Saturday.
Closed Sunday-Tuesday.

Peerless Italian cuisine from the only Lombardy-born chef in town, offered in a chill modern space with an open kitchen. This is the restaurant that reminds travelers of eating in Italy, run by a couple who trained up at Michelin-starred establishments, then gave Buffalo the next best thing.

DOG & PONY SALOON

2115 Seneca St., thedogandponysaloon.com,
716-322-0857
Hours: noon-midnight Tuesday-Thursday, noon-2:30
a.m. Friday, Saturday, 11:30 a.m.-10 p.m. Sunday.
Closed Monday.

South Buffalo neighborhood tavern with a thoroughly
modernized interior and menu. Alongside your wings
and fish fries, international cuisine and housemade
ingredients carry the day. Duck confit poutine,
Korean fried Brussels sprouts with gochujang sauce,
chicken Francese and yuzu salmon risotto hit.

THE DOVE

3002 Abbott Road, Orchard Park, thedoveny.com,
716-823-6680
Hours: 11:30 a.m.-2 p.m., 4:30 p.m.-8:30 p.m. Tuesday,
Thursday, 4:30 p.m.-8:30 p.m. Wednesday, Friday, Saturday.
Closed Sunday, Monday.

The epitome of old-school Italian-American dining.
With Sherry Davies out front and Dina Mattiello in
the kitchen, The Dove gives customers the sort of
soup-to-nuts restaurant experience many believed
extinct. Meatballs and sauce, salad, pasta fagioli, and
limoncello are gratis, part of the restaurant's old-fash-
ioned values.

Duff's Sheridan Patio

3651 Sheridan Drive, Amherst, duffswings.com,716-834-6234
Hours: 11 a.m.-9 p.m. Sunday-Thursday,
11 a.m.-10 p.m. Friday, Saturday.

My favorite place for wings, partly because I've enjoyed my single medium with fries there since 1983. Not to be confused with other locations bearing the Duff's nameplate.

Dulce Hogar Bakery

448 Oliver St., North Tonawanda, 716-525-1010
Hours:10 a.m.-10 p.m. Tuesday-Sunday. Closed Monday.

Try Colombian dishes like bandeja paisa, a carnivore Disneyland: fried pork belly, Colombian sausage, morcilla blood sausage, and steak, plus plantains, eggs, beans, and rice. Seafood stews, empanadas, and an entire lineup of baked sweets like caramel-cheese buns await.

Eagle House

5578 Main St., Williamsville, eaglehouseonline.com,
716-632-7669
Hours: 11:30 a.m.-9:30 p.m. Tuesday-Saturday.
Closed Sunday, Monday.

Historic restaurant serves old-school classics like
Welsh rarebit and chicken pot pie, plus a solid tavern
menu of salads, sandwiches, and wings. One of the
village's cozy wintertime pint-and-sandwich places
that can throw down at dinnertime.

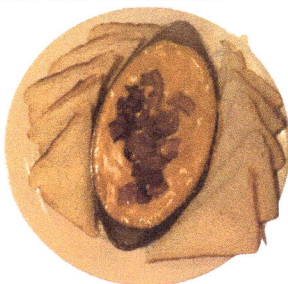

El Encanto

257 Virginia St., 716-322-1952
Hours: 11 a.m.-7 p.m. Monday, Tuesday, 11 a.m.-7 p.m.
Thursday, 11 a.m.-8 p.m. Friday, 12:30 p.m.-8 p.m. Saturday.
Closed Wednesday, Sunday.

Chill Puerto Rican restaurant with excellent versions of classics like pernil, empanadas, and plantains maduros. Ready-to-go pinchos like pastelillos and papas fritas await in the glass case beside the register. Get the boricua sampler to try an array of deep-fried treats.

Extra Extra Pizza

549 W Utica St., extraextrapizza.com, 716-248-2994
Hours: 5 p.m.-10 p.m. Monday-Thursday, noon-10 p.m.
Friday, Saturday. Closed Sunday.

Buffalo's best Brooklyn-style slice shop is a work-er-owned collective where you don't have to tip. Its pies have quickly become a weekly tradition, and not just for residents of the Five Points neighborhood.

FAIRBANKS

*460 Center St., Lewiston, fairbankslewiston.com,
716-405-7037*
Hours: 5 p.m.-9 p.m. Tuesday-Thursday, 5 p.m.-10
p.m. Friday, Saturday. Closed Sunday, Monday.

Billy Club owners opened an upscale modern American restaurant in a restored historic Lewiston building. Warm housemade Parker rolls, smoked salmon salad, and spaghetti alla chitarra are among standouts on the menu from Eleven Madison Park alum Matt Hirt.

FALAFEL BAR

3545 Sheridan Drive, Amherst, thefalafelbar.com,
716-436-7000
Hours:11 a.m.-8 p.m. Tuesday-Saturday, noon-8 p.m.
Sunday. Closed Monday.

Best-in-show falafel, hummus, and chicken shawarma
from Oded Rauvenpoor, the only Israeli chef in
town. Crispy chicken schnitzel speckled with sesame
seeds and hummus with lamb are standouts, but this
restaurant a mile from UB's Amherst Campus is also a
vegan haven, with four eggplant dishes alone.

FALAFEL HOUSE
BAKERY AND GRILL

1150 Hertel Ave., 716-259-8743
Hours: 11 a.m.-11 p.m. Sunday, Tuesday-Thursday,
11 a.m.-midnight Friday, Saturday. Closed Monday.

Beef kabab plate with rice and pickles and beef shawarma plate are my favorites at this Palestinian-Syrian
family restaurant. Loaded chicken shawarma fries are
a worthy stoner snack, while falafel, babaganoush, and
hummus feeds the need for plant-based life forms.

Family Thai

150 Babcock St., familythai-restaurant.com, 716-322-1102
Hours: 10 a.m.-9 p.m. Monday-Wednesday, Friday-Sunday.
Closed Thursday.
863 Tonawanda St., familythai-restaurant.com, 716-783-9285
Hours: 10 a.m.-9:30 p.m. Monday-Wednesday,
Friday-Sunday. Closed Thursday.

Try Burmese dishes like tea leaf salad, coconut noodle
soup, and egg curry, Thai specialties like larb, coconut
curries and yum woon sen seafood salad, and Chinese
soups like the pork-laden wonton noodle soup or
milky fried fish noodle soup. The dining rooms are
homey but the flavors never fail.

Farm Shop

235 B Lexington Ave. (entrance on Ashland)
Hours: 3 p.m.-7 p.m. Thursday, noon-5 p.m. Friday,
9 a.m.-5 p.m. Saturday, 10 a.m.-2 p.m. Sunday.
Closed Monday-Wednesday.

Cozy space designed as a discovery center for shoppers who value funneling their money back into the local economy. Buy Jenn Batt's Quokka Sweets ice creams. Or Savage Wheat Project's line of baked goods made without refined sugar, fat, or flour. But definitely meet Kelcey Gurtler, proprietor and "hype woman for everything local."

FARMERS & ARTISANS

4557 Main St., Amherst, farmersandartisans.com,
716-633-2830
Hours: 8 a.m.-6 p.m. Monday-Friday,
8 a.m.-5 p.m. Saturday. Closed Sunday.

Lowkey grocery of local and handmade goods, starting
with local vegetables, fruit, and flowers in season.
Great source for housemade bake-and-eat pies from
the freezer, along with meals, meats, dairy and locally
made ice cream. Stocks local beer, cider and kombucha.

THE FIRE SPOT

2829 River Road, Tonawanda, thefirespotrestaurant.com,
716-835-3473
Hours: Tuesday-Saturday 10 a.m.-9 p.m., noon-5 p.m.
Sunday. Closed Monday.

Buffalo Fire Department veteran Rodney Wilkinson's
retirement plan included taking his cooking skills to
the street. By the Tonawanda GM plant, his soul food
restaurant hits with chicken and waffles, breakfast all
day, fried seafood, shrimp and grits, and Wilkinson's
own fried chicken dish: baskets of fried chicken skin,
chicken chicharrones really, served with blue cheese
dressing.

FIVE POINTS BAKERY

44 Brayton St, fivepointsbakery.com, 716-884-8888
Hours: 8 a.m.-3 p.m. daily.

Whole-grain bakery grinds local wheat for wonders like whole-wheat cinnamon rolls and extra-sharp cheddar bread. Kevin and Melissa Garder turned a disused building into a community center that sells toast platters, the best sharp cheddar bread on the planet, and hosts live jazz in summer.

Forno Napoli

1280 Sweet Home Road, No. 105, Amherst, fornonapoliny. com, 716-636-9500
Hours: 4 p.m.-8 p.m. Tuesday-Thursday, noon-9 p.m. Friday, Saturday, 4 p.m.-8 p.m. Sunday. Closed Monday.

Reliable Neapolitan-style pies in a jumbo format, right across the street from UB's Amherst campus. Try the Felice, with San Marzano tomatoes, sausage, sweet and spicy peppers, buffalo mozzarella, or the Quattro Formaggi, with fresh mozzarella, gorgonzola, fontina, parmesan, and basil pesto.

Fortuna's

827 19th St., Niagara Falls,
fortunas.biz, 716-282-2252
Hours: 4 p.m.-8 p.m.
Wednesday, Thursday,
Sunday. 4 p.m.-9 p.m. Friday,
Saturday. Closed Monday,
Tuesday.

Housemade gnocchi and other pastas power the distinctive Italian-American menu. Try the Fortuna's-style parm, with American cheese instead of the usual broiled mozzarella. Get a plate of peppers half sweet, half hot, with cheese. Eat like people used to eat, and appreciate that Niagara Falls still has a place like Fortuna's.

FRANK GOURMET HOT DOGS

707 Kenmore Ave., Tonawanda, findfranknow.com,
716-322-5933
Hours: noon-7 p.m. Monday, noon-8 p.m.
Tuesday-Saturday. Closed Sunday.

Best-in-show burgers and fries, snazzied-up hot
dogs, and a fish fry so popular you have to schedule
pickup. Follow on socials to catch wind of coming
limited-time attractions like Frank's save-me-a-
pound pastrami, or Midwestern-style pork tender-
loin sandwiches the size of Frisbees.

GENE MCCARTHY'S
OLD FIRST WARD BREWING CO.

73 Hamburg St., genemccarthys.com, 716-855-8948
Kitchen hours: 11 a.m.-9 p.m.

One of the best places to catch old-school Buffalo tavern vibes with a solid menu of tavern food with character. The fish fries and Sheffield wings are justly famed, but the Reuben salad and portobello fingers with smoked blue cheese dressing also deserve attention.

Giancarlo's Sicilian Steakhouse

5110 Main St., Williamsville, giancarlossteakhouse.com,
716-650-5566
Hours: 5 p.m.-10 p.m. Monday-Thursday,
4 p.m.-10 p.m. Friday, Saturday. Closed Sunday.

Housemade pasta and adept service distinguishes Walker Center restaurant from most steak-and-pasta places. Try the calamari with red pepper agrodolce, rigatoni in vodka sauce, and whichever hunk of protein you fancy, and it's hard to go wrong.

GLEN PARK TAVERN

5507 Main St., Williamsville, glenparktavern.com, 716-626-9333
Hours: noon-9 p.m. Monday-Saturday. Closed Sunday.

One of the rare places where beef on kummelweck is still cut by hand, as pink or not as you prefer. Roast turkey is hand-carved too, making this historic tavern a stop on the Buffalo's best hits tour. The wings are solid, too, along with lobster bisque, french onion soup under a quilt of broiled cheese, and tavern standards like fish fries and fried bologna sandwiches.

GOLDEN HILL
ASIAN CUISINE

4001 Sheridan Drive, Amherst,
goldenhillasiancuisine.com,
716-631-7198
Hours: 11 a.m.-10 p.m. Monday,
Wednesday-Saturday,
noon-10 p.m. Sunday.
Closed Tuesday.

Menu includes solid Thai
and American Chinese dishes, but its glory is the
Chinese specialties. Standouts include crispy chicken
with fresh spicy pepper,
cold beef and tripe with
hot oil, and boiled fish
with pickled cabbage. Or
enjoy a soothing bowl-
for-two of West Lake
Beef Soup.

GONDOLA MACARONI PRODUCTS

1985 Niagara St.,
716-874-4280
Hours: 9:30 a.m.-4:30 p.m.
Monday-Saturday.
Closed Sunday.

Buffalo's retail fresh pasta center is three generations into the noodle business, making fresh pasta most days at the Niagara Street store. Fresh or frozen ravioli from cheese to lobster, fresh or dried fettucines, and fresh pasta sheets by the pound are some of the draws.

GRANGE COMMUNITY KITCHEN

22 Main St., Hamburg, grangecommunitykitchen.com, 716-648-0022

Hours: 4:30 p.m.-9:30 p.m. Wednesday, Thursday, 4:30 p.m.-10 p.m. Friday, 9 a.m.-2 p.m., 4:30 p.m.-10 p.m. Saturday, 9 a.m.-2 p.m. Sunday. Closed Monday, Tuesday.

Canny farm-to-table cooking, a full bakery with pastry chef, a well-used beehive pizza oven, and bespoke cocktails make this my No. 1 restaurant in all of Western New York. Chill servers, and food drawing from local riches and international ideas make reservations necessary.

GRAYLYNN

537 Main St., graylynnginbar.com, 716-370-0029,
Kitchen hours: 4 p.m.-10 p.m. Monday-Saturday. Bar:
until midnight Monday-Thursday,
1 a.m. Friday, Saturday.

European-leaning small plates, shares and sandwiches
menu in a bar that specializes in gin. Here you can find
one of the city's rare Scotch eggs, rum-butter escar-
got, and shoestring frites dusted with Old Bay. Porky
cheddar pasties and the fried mortadella sandwich are
heart-stoppers.

GYPSY PARLOR

376 Grant St., thegypsyparlor.com, 716-551-0001
Kitchen hours: 5 p.m.-11 p.m. daily.

Rehabbed neighborhood bar reflects community with
Puerto Rican and vegan offerings on its tavern menu.
The hearty house ramen, the banh mi poutine, along
with wings and haddock fish fries, make this spot a
default dinner site for neighbors.

HAYES SEAFOOD HOUSE

8900 Main St., Clarence, hayesseafoodhouse.com,
716-632-1772
Hours:11:45 a.m.- 8 p.m. Tuesday-Friday, 1:45 p.m.-8
p.m. Saturday. Closed Sunday, Monday.

The only dedicated seafood restaurant in town is
also a seafood market, started in 1877. The New-England-style crumb-coated shrimp and calamari are
irreplaceable. Weekly specials exploit the fresh fish in
its market for seafood entrees that make it the most
reliable place in town when you just want a nice piece
of fish.

Hilltop Restaurant

4206 Lake Ave., Lockport, thehilltoprestaurant.com,
716-433-7060
Hours: 2 p.m.-9 p.m. Tuesday-Thursday, 10 a.m.-11 p.m.
Friday, 2 p.m.-10 p.m. Saturday. Closed Sunday, Monday.

Entrees come with soup or salad, and fresh house-made bread jazzed-up butter. Cheeseburger soup and creamy New England clam chowder with potatoes speak to owners Anthony and Crystal Conrad's diner family roots. Try the bacon-wrapped Better Than Mama's Meatloaf and variety of housemade potsticker dumplings.

Holy Feast

3198 Main St., 716-579-5412
Hours: 6 p.m.-midnight Sunday, Monday-Wednesday, 6 p.m.-4 a.m. Thursday-Saturday.

Halal fast food from a truck in a gas station parking lot hits the spot deep into the night in University Heights, including until 4 a.m. Thursday-Saturday. Try the paneer burger, a hefty slab of cheese battered, deep-fried, sauced and served on a bun.

HOME TASTE

3106 Delaware Ave., Kenmore, 716-322-0088
Hours: 5 p.m.-9:30 p.m. Tuesday, Wednesday,
11 a.m.-9:30 p.m. Thursday-Sunday. Closed Monday.

Dumplings, noodles, and potatoes are strengths of
this Northern Chinese restaurant, but salads are
standouts too: try the celery with tofu skin. Crispy
fried cod, noodle soups, shredded potatoes with chile
and vinegar, and pork-stuffed omelet all offer ways to
expand your Chinese culinary vocabulary.

Hot Mama's Canteen

12 Military Road, hotmamascanteen.com, 716-783-8222
Hours: 5 p.m.-1 a.m. Tuesday-Thursday, 5 p.m.-4 a.m. Friday,
Saturday, 4 p.m.-midnight Sunday, 5 p.m-2 a.m. Monday

Double-dipped housemade chicken tenders, smashburgers with house-cut fries, and softball-sized stuffed
arancini are stars of the late-night menu. Vintage
shuffleboard, pool, and darts are standard amuse-
ments, with a diverse entertainment calendar.

HOUSE OF SANDWICH

800 Tonawanda St.,
716-342-2684
Hours: 8 a.m.-6 p.m.
Monday-Wednesday, 8 a.m.-8
p.m. Thursday-Saturday,
9 a.m.-6 p.m Sunday.

Sandwiches that will fill a day's calorie needs are the specialty of this Riverside Puerto Rican spot. The pernil and Cubano are formidable, but tripletas of grilled chicken, pastrami, and roast pork are my jam.

Hydraulic Hearth

716 Swan St., hydraulichearth. com, 716-248-2216
Hours: 4 p.m.-9 p.m. Tuesday, Wednesday, 4 p.m.-10 p.m. Thursday, 4 p.m.-11 p.m. Friday, Saturday. Closed Sunday, Monday.

Opened 12 years ago in the redeveloped Larkin Square neighborhood, it's a brick oven pizza joint and full-service bar with a tiki cocktail strong suit. Casual help-yourself atmosphere, you get your own water and napkins, but the pizzas are delivered straight to your table.

Imperial Pizza

035 Abbott Road, imperialpizzabuffalo.com,
716-825-3636
1661 Main St., imperialpizzabuffalo.com,
716-508-2261
Hours: 11 a.m.-10 p.m. daily.

Founded by former Bocce employees, Imperial stands tall among Buffalo pie purveyors. Heavy cheese, cup-and-char pepperoni, slices that will never fold. South Buffalo mothership includes dining room with full bar and copious television screens for watch parties. Two slices of cheese and pep forever.

Inchin's Bamboo Garden

5415 Sheridan Drive, Amherst, 716-580-3032
Hours: 11 a.m.-2:30 p.m., 4 p.m.-9 p.m. Monday,
Wednesday, Thursday, 11 a.m.-2:30 p.m., 4 p.m.-9:30
p.m. Friday, 11:30 a.m.-2:30 p.m., 4 p.m.-9:30 p.m.
Saturday, 11:30 a.m.-3 p.m., 4 p.m.-9 p.m.

Indian and Chinese-Indian dishes from a sprawling
menu, in a roomy plaza dining space with a full bar.
Try lamb dumplings, chicken dumplings "hot pot"
style, Malaysian roti canai with chicken curry, and In-
do-Chinese specialties like crispy chili corn and paneer
65.

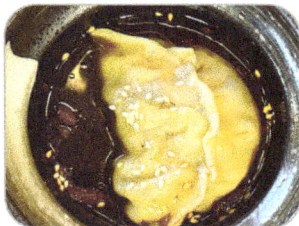

ILIO DiPAOLO'S
RESTAURANT

3785 South Park Ave., Blasdell, iliodipaolos.com, 716-825-3675
Hours: 3 p.m.-9 p.m. Wednesday, Thursday, noon-9 p.m.
Friday, 2 p.m.-9 p.m. Saturday, 2 p.m.-8 p.m. Sunday.

Wrestling champion Ilio DiPaolo's restaurant has
its own legacy now, after his children fed another
generation. Chicken parinello (prosciutto, roasted red
peppers, spinach, asiago) caught my fancy here. If you
have the guts to consider tripe, the tender, funky bites
in tomato sauce are simply soulful.

Inizio

534 Elmwood Ave., inizio716.com, 716-424-1008
Hours: 5 p.m-9 p.m. Tuesday-Saturday.
Closed Sunday, Monday.

Nine or ten varieties of housemade pasta, sauced
expertly, are the flagship attraction. But small plates
like espresso-crusted hangar steak and broccoli rabe
with garlic and almonds can be a meal by themselves.
"Everything by hand," is the restaurant's motto, and
the craft comes through on the plate.

INTERNATIONAL HOUSE

617 Main St., internationalhousebuffalo.com,
716-248-2622
Hours: 11:30 a.m.-8:30 p.m. Tuesday-Saturday.
Bar open until midnight.

Four international restaurants and a bar run by Pink Flamingo founder Mark Supples inhabit a block-wide room lined with custom artwork celebrating Buffalo's immigrant heritage. Buffalo's only Filipino and Ethiopian restaurants, plus Burmese-Thai and bubble tea, and Mexican tacos make this Theater District spot a happy place for people with children and diverse groups.

Iron Tail Tavern

802 Elmwood Ave., irontailtavern.com, 716-815-2345
Hours: 4 p.m.-10 p.m. Monday, Thursday, 4 p.m.-11
p.m. Friday, 11 a.m.-11 p.m. Saturday, 11 a.m.-9 p.m.
Sunday. Closed Tuesday, Wednesday.

Veteran chef Andrew Berger presents a Spanish-in-
spired menu of small plates and entrees. Highlights
include a rare appearance of patatas bravas, fried
potatoes with smoky pimenton and creamy garlic
sauces. Grilled sirloin with chimichurri, seafood stew,
and grilled prawns are all good reasons to stop by for
dinner.

JASMINE THAI

1330 Niagara Falls Blvd., Tonawanda, jasthai.com,
716-838-3011
Hours: noon-8 p.m. daily.

Area's longest-tenured Thai restaurant hits with standards like chicken in peanut sauce, duck curry, and pad thai, but also offers the only mee krob in town, puffy rice noodles wok-fired in caramel until they're like Cracker Jacks for adults.

JAY'S ARTISAN PIZZERIA

2872 Delaware Ave., Kenmore, jaysbuffalo.com
Hours: 4 p.m.-8 p.m. Tuesday-Saturday.
Closed Sunday, Monday.

Internationally acclaimed pizzeria specializes in Neapolitan pies, with leopard-spotted corniciones from the intense heat, and Detroit-style, baked in a pan that leaves each slice cheese-rimmed. Choose from standards like the prizewinning 'nduja, with dabs of Calabrian salami, the funghi, with truffled cream, or a seasonal special.

K Dara Noodle Bar

110 Pearl St., kdara.net, 716-939-2002
Hours: 11 a.m.-2 p.m. Tuesday, 11 a.m.-9 p.m. Wednesday,
Thursday, 11 a.m.-9:30 p.m. Friday, 4:30 p.m.-9:30 p.m.
Saturday. Closed Sunday, Monday.

Today the best broth in Buffalo can be found in the
basement of the Dun Building, on Pearl Street. There,
Laotian-American chef Vathanathavone "2-2" Inthalasy
offers rakish cooking, with ecstatic broths, enticing
textures, and a menu of finely honed favorites that make
you want to let loose and suck the marrow out of life.

KITH & KIN
BAKESHOP & BISTRO

5850 S. Transit Road, Lockport, kkbakeshop.com,
716-471-3305
Hours: 11 a.m.-8 p.m. Tuesday-Saturday.
Closed Sunday, Monday.

Parents with children with celiac run full-spectrum bakery and restaurant. That means breakfast, lunch, and dinner risk-free for people with celiac, right down to beer and wine. Plus takeaways like frozen pizza crust, pancake mix, and cinnamon buns.

KONBINI BUFFALO

523 Main St., kombinibuffalo.com,
Hours: 11 a.m.-2 p.m. Tuesday-Thursday: 11 a.m.-2
p.m., 6 p.m.-9 p.m. Friday, noon-7 p.m. Saturday.
Closed Sunday, Monday.

Hidden inside the 500 block of Main Street in a
corridor of small shops, Konbini makes the Japanese
stuffed rice balls called onigiri and ramen with housemade noodles, one plate or bowl at a time. Uemboshi
onigiri - stuffed with salted plums that pack Warheads
pucker power - make a rousing bite. The ramen just
plain smacks, especially the tantan ramen, inspired by
Chinese peanut noodles.

Kostas Family Restaurant

1561 Hertel Ave., kostasfamilyrestaurant.com,
716-838-5225
Hours: 7 a.m.-9 p.m. Monday-Saturday, 8 a.m.-9 p.m.
Sunday.

Grand-daddy of Buffalo Greek diners still offers
Hellenic soul food like horta, dandelion greens, and
reliable roast lamb dinners. Pancakes, salads, omelets,
and gyro-souvlaki combos are probably the most popular items. Still the most Greek restaurant in Buffalo.

KUNI'S

226 Lexington Ave., kunisbuffa-lo.com, 716-881-3800
Hours: Hours: 5 p.m.-9 p.m. Tuesday-Thursday, 5 p.m.-10 p.m. Friday, Saturday. Closed Sunday, Monday.

Want sushi Japanese style? Go see Thaviesak "Vic" Nachampassak, who worked with Kuni Sato before the founder retired. Sushi plus dishes like: hamachi kama, grilled yellowtail collar, or gintara, black cod marinated in sweet miso and grilled. Even a fish fry, in panko crumbs, with gossamer slaw.

La Casa de Sabores

1 Letchworth St.,
716-370-1484
Hours: 11 a.m.-8:30 p.m.
Monday, Tuesday, Thurs-
day-Saturday, 11 a.m.-6 p.m.
Sunday. Closed Wednesday.

Dominican take-out restaurant offers savory
rib-sticking meal boxes dished up to order on the
buffet line, or cooked-to-order selections. Tres
golpes, "three hits,"
tops mashed plantains
and pickled onions
with fried salami, fried
cheese, plus a fried egg.

La Divina Tacos

2896 Delaware Ave., Kenmore, 716-447-8989
Hours: 11 a.m.-8 p.m. daily.
617 Main St., 716-248-2622
Hours: 10:30 a.m.-8:30 p.m. Tuesday-Saturday.
Closed Sunday, Monday.

Kenmore taco standard opened downtown at International House. Both locations offer tacos, burritos, quesadillas, and nachos in al pastor, birria, and pork. Plus a salsa bar where you can personalize your purchases to your liking, and a rainbow of Jarritos.

La Flor Bakery

544 Niagara St., laflorbuffalo.com, 716-812-0187
Hours: 7 a.m.-7 p.m. Monday-Saturday, 7 a.m.-6 p.m. Sunday.

Puerto Rican steamtable specials like smothered pork
chops and pernil with rice and pigeon peas alongside
a full bakery case of boricua sweets like tres leches
cake and guava turnovers dusted with powdered
sugar.

La Oaxaqueña Taqueria

4152 W. Main Street Road, Batavia, 585-219-4108
Hours: 11 a.m.-7 p.m. Monday, Thursday-Sunday.
Closed Tuesday, Wednesday.

One mile from the Batavia Thruway exit, Nancy Rosario's restaurant offers an array of tacos, with al pastor (chile, pork, pineapple) and carnitas (roast pork) among standouts. Posole, pork-hominy-tripe-chile soup, is a weekend special. Also shop Monte Alban II, a Mexican grocery, in the same plaza, run by the same family.

Lexington Co-op

807 Elmwood Ave., lexington.coop, 716-886-2667
1678 Hertel Ave., lexington.coop, 716-886-0024
Hours: 7 a.m.-11 p.m. daily

Ready-to-eat sandwiches, salads, and soups scratch-made daily have made the community-owned markets on Elmwood and Hertel one of Buffalo's most reliable cafeterias. Vegan, gluten-free, and organic choices abound, along with vegetables, fruit, meat, and bread from local producers.

Lin Asian Market

929 Tonawanda St., 716-948-9235
Hours: 9 a.m.-8 p.m. daily.

Burmese and Southeast Asian market with lunchtime
grab-and-go meals of grilled meat, noodle dishes,
and mohinga soup at cash register. Extensive freezer
selections of meat, fish, and vegetables, plus fresh
vegetables and herbs.

LITTLE LAMB HOT POT

3188 Sheridan Drive, Amherst, 716-834-0218
Hours: 4 p.m.-9:30 p.m. Monday-Thursday,
11 a.m.-9:30 p.m. Friday-Sunday.

The format is "choose your own adventure," with a
delightfully diverse array of options. Pick a meat and
a broth, then go scouting in two categories. What else
will go into the pot? What will make your dipping
sauce? If you want to cook dinner with friends and
pay someone else to clean up, this is an ideal night
out.

LLOYD TACO FACTORY

1503 Hertel Ave., whereslloyd.com, 716-863-9781
Hours: 11 a.m.-11 p.m. Monday-Thursday, 11
a.m.-midnight Friday, Saturday. Closed Sunday.
5933 Main St., whereslloyd.com, 716-863-9781
Hours: 11 a.m.-11 p.m. Monday-Saturday.
Closed Sunday.

Burritos and El Camino rice bowls, or tricked-out
nachos with housemade queso are my favorite way to
enjoy Lloyd's taco fillings. Pork, beef, chicken, crispy
fish and fried tofu can feed just about everyone. Also,
Lloyd sells its house-ground masa corn dough, and its
housemade tortillas.

LOUIE'S DELI & IMPORTS

8202 Main St., Clarence, louiesdeli.com, 716-632-4906
Hours: 9:30 a.m.-5 p.m. Monday-Saturday.
Closed Sunday.

If you miss Little Italy sandwich shops, consider a place that fries its own cutlets for sandwiches, bakes several styles of stuffed breads available by the slice, and offers a broad array of salads and meal elements by the pound. Try the Italian Club (grilled capicola, provolone, turkey) or Cleopatra (marinated eggplant, asiago cheese, sun-dried tomatoes, romaine, vinaigrette).

Louisiana Cookery

8671 Lake Road, Barker, the-louisiana-cookery.square.site,
716-727-4533
Hours: 4 p.m.-8 p.m. Wednesday, noon-4 p.m. Thursday, 4 p.m.-8 p.m. Friday, Saturday.
Closed Sunday-Tuesday.

Righteous New Orleans cuisine outpost in northern Niagara County, a mile from Lake Ontario. Heartfelt renditions of andouille and chicken gumbo, shrimp and grits, fried catfish, jambalaya, crawfish etouffee, and more Cajun-Creole and Southern comfort food.

LOVEJOY PIZZERIA

1244 E. Lovejoy St., lovejoypizza.com, 716-891-9233
Hours: 11 a.m.-8:30 p.m. Monday-Thursday, 11 a.m.-
9:30 p.m. Friday, Saturday, noon-9:30 p.m. Sunday.
900 Main St., lovejoypizza.com, 716-883-2323
Hours: 10:30 a.m.-7:30 p.m. Tuesday-Saturday. Closed
Sunday, Monday.

Topflight Buffalo-style pizza and wings from a steady
operator. Main Street location feeds the Medical
Campus, while the original location feeds Lovejoy and
environs. The lunch special of two slices of cheese and
pep plus four wings is a life-saver.

Lucky Day Whiskey Bar

320 Pearl St.., luckydaywhiskey-
bar.com, 716-322-0547
Kitchen Hours: 4 p.m.-10 p.m.
Tuesday-Thursday,
4 p.m.-11 p.m. Friday, Saturday. Closed Sunday, Monday.

Great deals abound at happy hour, 4 p.m.-6 p.m. daily.
A $25 steak frites and a $6 cheeseburger made with a
patty that's half beef, half bacon are epic deals. A $6
fried chicken sandwich and vegetarian mushroom
cheesesteak follow suit.
If you tipple, $6 cock-
tails made by a profes-
sional are on tap too.
There is also a dinner
menu.

Mahar Moe

3668 Delaware Ave., Tonawanda, maharmoeasiancuisine.com, 716-331-3336
Hours: 11 am-10 pm Tuesday-Saturday, noon-10 pm Sunday. Closed Monday.

Owner Ping Fa Li dishes up tickets to Hong Kong, Chengdu, and Kuala Lumpur, alongside rock-solid bargains in General Tso and the usual suspects. Plenty of Sichuan Chinese and American Chinese Rare-for-Buffalo Malaysian dishes like kam heong fish or chicken, and Hong Kong Typhoon Shelter Style, shrimp hidden in a drift of savory breadcrumbs.

Maizal Mexican Kitchen
& Mezcaleria

4840 N. French Road, East Amherst,
maizalmexicankitchen.com, 716-428-5683
Hours: 4 p.m.-8 p.m. Monday-Thursday,
11 a.m.-9 p.m. Friday, Saturday, 11 a.m.-7 p.m. Sunday.

Oaxacan chef Leonel Rosario has more moles on his
Maizal menu, foreshadowing his Day of the Dead
dinner featuring seven versions of the Mexican sim-
mer sauces. Two moles, poblano and verde, are on the
menu year-round. Standouts include birria eggrolls,
skillet-bronzed queso fundido, a mezcal library, and
Oaxacan tlayudas.

Manito Taco Shop

3958 Lockport Olcott Road, Lockport, 716-697-6085
Hours: 11 a.m.-8 p.m. Tuesday-Sunday. Closed Monday.

Taco fillings basic and advanced (cecina adobada, lengua, tripa) that you can doctor up at an extensive toppings bar of salsas, herbs, and pickles. They're served up by a hustling team led by Manito Gonzalez, a cheery taquero with a personality as big as the flavors. My spot when I feel like hammering some queso carne asada fries. Honored as Top 100 Yelp spot in 2024.

MARBLE + RYE

112 Genesee St., Buffalo NY,
marbleandrye.net, 716-853-1390
Hours: 5 p.m.-9 p.m. Monday, Wednesday, Thursday, 5
p.m.-10 p.m. Friday, Saturday. Closed Tuesday, Sunday.

Buffalo's most cash-effective happy hour with killer vegan apps, my favorite cheeseburger, and Detroit-style pizza are top reasons to visit. Housemade pasta with bolognese and double smashburgers on housemade rolls are perennial favorites. Cocktails are another bright spot, bespoke drams served in cool retro glassware.

MAYBACK'S DELI

1598 Niagara Falls Blvd., Tonawanda, 716-835-0115
Hours: 10 a.m.-8 p.m. Monday-Saturday.
Closed Sunday.

Across the street from a dismal lineup of underwhelming franchise eats, sandwich superspot offers all-day breakfast sandwiches, stinger subs, old-school club sandwiches, and grilled tuna melts. Call ahead for quicker service, or order and have a seat in the dining area.

MILLER'S THUMB
BAKERY & CAFE

258 Highland Parkway, Tonawanda, millersthumbbakery.com,
716-364-6362

Hours: 7 a.m.-3 p.m. Wednesday-Friday, 8 a.m.-2 p.m.
Saturday, Sunday.

Artisanal bread from an award-winning veteran baker
who mills all his own flour, with remarkable results
in flavor and texture. Bread, rolls, cookies, cakes, and
seasonal delicacies have the Tonawanda shop on the
map of croissant hunt-
ers and danish fan-
ciers — even kouign
amann nerds.

wonderful
loaf
soft, buttery
country loaf
$5.95 | half $3.00

Mira

1081 Elmwood Ave., mirabuffalo.com, 716-783-7000
Hours: 5 p.m.-9 p.m. Tuesday, 5 p.m.-10 p.m. Wednesday,
Thursday, 5 p.m.-11 p.m. Friday, 9 a.m.-2:30 p.m., 5 p.m.-11
p.m. Saturday. Closed Sunday, Monday.

New Elmwood anchor offers broadly Mediterranean
menu from Grange Community Kitchen owners. Led
by Manuel Ocasio, the wood-grill-centered kitch-
en turns out plates of
simple classics in waves
of mezze and big plates
like whole grilled fish,
each elevated by refined
technique.

Mojo Market

3030 Delaware Ave., Kenmore, mojomarket.com,
716-874-6656
Hours: 8:30 a.m.-3:30 p.m. Tuesday-Saturday.
Closed Sunday, Monday.

The breakfast and lunch spot you wish was on your block. Housemade bread, local produce, and real table service. Egg and cheddar cheese on a housemade English muffin costs less than an Egg McMuffin, salads packed with protein, and stylish sandwiches abound. Frozen heat-and-eat offerings join a pantry section with Buffalo food specialties.

MONTE'S GROCERY DELI

413 Swan St., 716-854-3228
Hours: 9:30 a.m.-7 p.m. Monday-Friday, 10 a.m.-7
p.m. Saturday. Closed Sunday.

Puerto Rican steamtable operation has folks lining
up for pastelillos and plates at lunch and dinner
hours. The pernil is estimable, but Thursday's special
of bistec encebollado, beef simmered with sofrito, es
muy rico.

MORIARTY MEATS AND CAFE BAR MORIARTY

1650 Elmwood Ave., moriartymeats.com, 716-239-8465
Cafe hours: 11 a.m.-2 p.m. Wednesday, 11 a.m.-4 p.m.
Thursday-Saturday. Closed Sunday-Tuesday.
Butcher shop hours 10 a.m.-6 p.m. Tuesday-Friday,
10 a.m.-4 p.m. Saturday.

French-trained butcher offering diverse cuts of local
beef, lamb, and pork, plus well as homemade sausages,
smoked meats, and prepared foods. Here's the picanha,
guanciale, duck confit, and more. Cafe offers soulful
small, medium, and meal-sized plates, including its best-
in-show boeuf on weck, my favorite version yet.

Mulberry Italian Ristorante

64 Jackson Ave., Lackawanna, mulberryitalianristorante.com,
716-822-4292
Hours: 11:30 a.m.-2:30 p.m., 4 p.m.-8:30 p.m.
Monday-Saturday. Closed Sunday.

Housemade pastas and big-time Italian-American favorites served by an experienced crew make reservations smart at this essential Lackawanna restaurant. Showstoppers like the short rib agnolotti, sprawling veal cutlet parmesan, and Tre White's spicy BBQ wings elevate dinner to a night among the stars.

NANA PERUVIAN KITCHEN

21 Prospect St., Fredonia, 716-401-3048
Hours: 11 a.m.-8 p.m. Wednesday-Friday, 11 a.m.-9 p.m.
Saturday, 11 a.m.-8 p.m. Sunday.
Closed Monday, Tuesday.

Fredonia got a real Peruvian restaurant when Nana
opened in a former tavern off the main drag. Brilliant
ceviche spiked with lime, chile, and cumin, aji de
gallina creamed chicken, and lomo soltado, a stir-fry
of beef, tomatoes, french fries, and more, with thrill
Peruvian fans, and impress just about everyone else.

Natalie's
Mediterranean Eatery

807 ½ Millersport Highway, Amherst, 716-446-9715
Hours: 10 a.m.-6 p.m. Monday-Friday,
11 a.m.-3 p.m. Saturday. Closed Sunday.

At this second-generation family restaurant, Mediterranean means comfort food with deep Levantine roots,
like chickpea-and-tahini hummus, eggplant-and-tahini
babaganoush, and felafel chickpea fritters. Housemade
soups like chicken lemon rice and vegan offerings like
gazpacho are everyday standards.

Nellai Banana Leaf

4303 Transit Road, Clarence,
nellaibananaleaf.com,
716-276-3786
Hours: 11:30 a.m. to 2:30
p.m., 5 p.m.-9:30 p.m. Tuesday-Saturday, 5 p.m.-8:30 p.m.
Sunday. Closed Monday.

Chettinad Indian cuisine, with more sour, garlicky
character, plus South Indian specialties like dosa, idly,
and uttapam, rules here. Standouts here include eggplant in tamarind garlic gravy, marina beach sundal
chickpea-mango-coconut salad, and chilli parotta,
stir-fried croutons in smoky sauce.

Nephew's BBQ

1125 Tonawanda St., 716-322-1800
Hours: 11 a.m.-7 p.m.
Thursday, 11 a.m.-10 p.m.
Friday, Saturday,
noon-5 p.m. Sunday

Lee Smith's famed grilled spare ribs, offered by his nephew, plus fried seafood and soul food like collard greens with cornbread, plus a full bar. Category note: These are grilled ribs, meant to be gnawed, not the long slow-smoked type with meat that slides off the bone.

NIAGARA CAFE

525 Niagara St., 716-885-2233
Hours: 11 a.m.-8 p.m. Tuesday-Saturday.
Closed Sunday, Monday.

The lunch specials at Buffalo's oldest Puerto Rican restaurant make it a busy place around noon. There's no more table service, but customers can sit down and eat. Pernil and rice with pigeon peas, plus beans is my go-to almuerzo, plus an order of maduros, plantains fried to caramel lushness.

NINE & NIGHT THAI CUISINE

414 Amherst St., nineandnight.com, 716-541-7963
Hours: 11 a.m.-8 p.m. Monday-Thursday, 11 a.m.-9 p.m.
Friday, Saturday. Closed Sunday.

Thai favorites like fried-egg-topped pad ka pow and bracing green papaya salad are enough reason to visit. Restaurateur Htay Naing also offers specialties worth meeting like black pepper beef and fried ramen coconut noodle, plus mango sticky rice for dessert.

OG Dumpling House

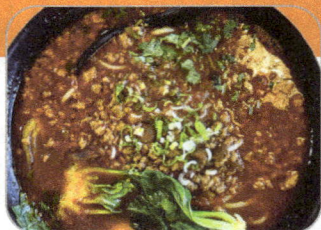

1400 Niagara Falls Blvd., Tonawanda, ogdumpling-houseny.com, 716-259-8657
Hours: 11 a.m.-9 p.m. Monday-Thursday, Sunday,
11 a.m.-10 p.m. Friday, Saturday.

Gigantic bowls with huge Chinese flavors like spicy
brisket soup and dan dan noodles with pork are excellent reasons to visit. Try vegetable bao, fried dumplings, and a version of Shanghaiese soup dumplings,
xiao long bao, that are lovely if you're not too picky.

Olisi's NY Pizza

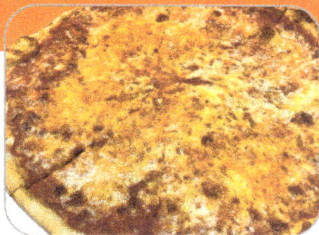

2352 Sheridan Drive, Tonawanda, olisisny.com,
716-837-6767
Hours: 10 a.m.-8:30 p.m. Sunday-Thursday, 10 a.m.-9
p.m. Friday, Saturday.

The first choice of downstaters looking for a Noo
Yawk slice is actually run by Albanians, but their pizza
is so on point that no one cares. It's busy enough at
peak times that you should call several hours before
you want your pie, unless you don't mind waiting.

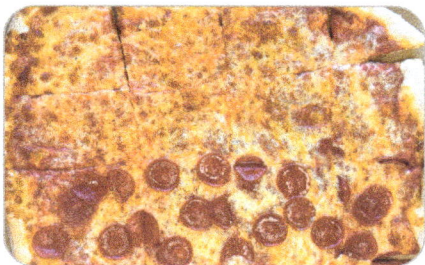

ORALIA

403 Main St. Suite 109, oralia716.square.site, 716-598-1062
Hours: 7:30 a.m.-3 p.m. Tuesday-Friday.
Closed Saturday-Monday.

Breakfast tacos in regular and vegan styles, house-made salsas, and abundant space in peace and quiet in Lafayette Square are some of Oralia's draws. Then there's the cheese-stuffed roasted poblano chiles, and more offerings from Jessica Melisz, with an assist from her partner's madre.

Pattaya Street Food

617 Main St., pattaya-street-food.square.site, 716-335-6816
Hours: 10:30 a.m.-8:30 p.m. Tuesday-Saturday.
Closed Sunday, Monday.

Elizabeth Sher brings her Burmese and Thai cuisine back to 617 Main St. as International House. That includes coconut milk curry chicken noodle soup, green papaya salad, tea leaf salad, and lotus flower cookies.

PARKER'S GREAT BRITISH INSTITUTION

495 Aero Drive, Cheektowaga, parkersgbi.com, 716-823-3772
Hours: 9 a.m.-5 p.m. Monday, 9 a.m.-4 p.m. Tuesday-Friday,
10 a.m.-2 p.m. Saturday. Closed Sunday.

Duck into the semi-hidden British foods emporium, and you'll find the characteristic staples of English diets - sauces, sweets, beverages - plus a whole raft of English-style pies, sausage rolls, and more, all made in the same building.

PEKING QUICK ONE

359 Somerville Ave., Tonawanda, 716-381-8730
Hours: 11 a.m.-10 p.m. Wednesday-Monday. Closed Tuesday.

The Chinese-American and Chinese-Chinese menus both hit here. Try the slip cucumber, poached tripe in chile oil, or crispy sliced fish. Chinese omelets and shredded chile potatoes may expand horizons. Your food will arrive in takeout containers, but that just makes it easier to bring the rest home for lunch tomorrow.

PHAM'S KITCHEN

2940 Union Road, Cheektowaga, phamskitchen716.com,
716-901-7663
Hours: 9 a.m.-8 p.m. Monday-Friday, 9 a.m.-9 p.m.
Saturday. Closed Sunday.

My favorite Vietnamese place for baking banh mi
loaves fresh every morning, filling them with pickled
vegetables, liver pate, mayonnaise, and three types of
cold cuts, all housemade, for $7.75. The pork chop
plate and bun cha with pickled green papaya are
definitive.

PHO DOLLAR

322 W. Ferry St., phodollarvietnamese.com,
716-768-0049
Hours: 11 a.m.-8:45 p.m. Monday-Saturday,
11 a.m.-7:45 p.m. Sunday.

Solid Vietnamese place with praiseworthy pho, bun
bo hue, and goi ga, the salad of chicken tossed with
gossamer shredded cabbage and carrot. Get the grilled
pork and egg on rice for a real diner-level stick-to-the-
ribs meal.

Picasso's Pizza

6812 Transit Road, Amherst, picassospizza.net,
716-631-0222
2193 Union Road, West Seneca, picassospizza.net,
716-668-1111
5413 Broadway, Lancaster, picassospizza.net,
716-684-4404
Hours: 11 a.m.-9 p.m. Sunday-Thursday, 11 a.m.-10
p.m. Friday, Saturday.
4154 McKinley Parkway, Blasdell, picassospizza.net,
716-202-1313
Hours: 11 a.m.-8 p.m. Sunday-Thursday, 11 a.m.-9
p.m. Friday, Saturday.

Classic Buffalo pizza, by the two-cheese-and-pep-
with-drink combo or party sheets to feed the crowds.
Wings, subs, fries, the whole shebang.

Pinoy Boi

617 Main St, pinoyboibuffalo.square.site
Hours: 10:30 a.m.-8:30 p.m. Tuesday-Saturday.
Closed Sunday, Monday.

Buffalo's only Filipino restaurant reopened at International House, 617 Main St. in April, along with its companions. That means pork sisig and lumpia, beef kare-kare, lechón roast pork belly, and ube Basque cheesecake, for starters.

PITA GOURMET

Niagara Falls: 1930 Military Road, 716-298-8015
Orchard Park: 3144 Orchard Park Road, 716-599-1411
Hamburg: 5565 Camp Road, 716-599-1300
East Amherst: 6031 Transit Road, 716-799-1222
Amherst: 3122 Sheridan Drive, 716-599-1111
Williamsville (Depew): 6733 Transit Road, Suite 600,
716-633-3303
Hours: 10:30 a.m.-9 p.m. Monday-Saturday. Closed Sunday.

Quick-serve Greek done right, with chicken souvlaki
made of tenders and beef grilled to order. Patient
counterpeople help you doctor up your salad or souvlaki with 25 vegetable, cheese, and sauce accents.

PUBLIC ESPRESSO

391 Washington St., 716-367-9971
2178 Seneca St., 716-491-9013
448 Elmwood Ave., 716-235-8202
publicespresso.com
Hours: 7 a.m.-2 p.m. daily.

Roasting its own beans in Buffalo since 2013, Public
also offers bagel sandwiches, salads, egg-topped hash
bowls in sweet potato and chorizo spiced pork, and
granola all day. Doughnuts and crullers in flavors like
salted caramel also beckon.

QUENELLE

*341 Franklin St., quenellebuffa-
lo.com, 716-322-0042*
Hours: 4 p.m.-10 p.m. Monday,
4 p.m.-1 a.m. Thursday-Saturday, 11 a.m.-2:30 p.m., 4
p.m.-10 p.m. Sunday. Closed
Tuesday, Wednesday.

French restaurant opened last year in former Rue
Franklin space. Dinner and Sunday brunch follow the
French canon, with frog's legs, boeuf bourguignon,
and of course quenelles, fish dumplings in lobster
sauce.

Raha Coffee House

370 Amherst St., rahacoffee-house.com, 716-615-5555
Hours: 8 a.m.-10 p.m. Monday-Thursday, 8 a.m.-midnight Friday, Saturday, 10 a.m.-10 p.m. Sunday.

Yemeni coffee operation serving full lineup of standard lattes but also Arabic blends involving cinnamon, cardamom, coffee hulls, and other twists. Honeycomb pastries and more sweets are available. Pots of coffee meant for lingering over with friends and a cozy interior has made Raha a late-night magnet for people who want to hang out in a non-alcohol-centered third place.

REMEDY HOUSE

429 Rhode Island St., remedyhouse.co, 716-248-2155
Hours: Hours: 7 a.m.-9 p.m. Monday-Saturday,
7 a.m.-3 p.m. Sunday.

Five Points coffeehouse offers a definitive egg on a
roll, along with a complete catalogue of coffee drinks
and alcoholic eye-openers. The broader food menu
includes savories like jamon beurre, pan-fried white
cheddar macaroni and cheese, and oyster mushroom
tartine.

Risa's Deli & Catering

285 Delaware Ave., 716-842-6860
Hours: 7:30 a.m. to 3 p.m. weekdays

The only source for kosher-style deli sandwiches, chicken soup with matzo ball, and bubbe-formed knishes is hidden in anodyne bank building. Stop by for a pastrami with a schmear, a Cel-Ray, and a bowl of sweet-and-sour cabbage soup. (Read review)

Rizzo's House of Parm

2 Ridgeway Road, Ridgeway, Ont., Canada, rizzoshouseof-parm.com, 905-894-0555

Hours: 4 p.m.-9:30 p.m. Monday-Thursday, 4 p.m.-10 p.m. Friday, 2 p.m.-10 p.m. Saturday, 2 p.m.-9:30 p.m.

Restaurant and TV star Matty Matheson fell in love with Italian-American standards in Buffalo, and his just-over-the-bridge restaurant is upgraded homage to its cheese-covered glories. The parms, the pastas, the upgraded wedge are money. Reservations required.

ROYAL FAMILY RESTAURANT

1320 Sheridan Drive, Tonawanda,
theroyalfamilyrestaurant.com, 716-873-0056
Hours: 6 a.m.-9 p.m. Tuesday-Saturday, 6 a.m.-3 p.m. Sunday.
Closed Monday.

Housemade gyro the Greek way, marinated pork and chicken sliced off a spit, is testament to the old-school diner spirit here. The Royal is the only version in town. It's my favorite spot for a Friday fish fry when folks are waiting an hour in the usual places.

Sato Ramen

3268 Main St., satorestaurantgroup.square.site,
716-835-7286

Hours: 11 a.m.-8 p.m. Tuesday-Thursday, 11 a.m.-8:30 p.m. Friday, Saturday, noon-8 p.m. Sunday, Monday.

Ramen cubbyhole across Main Street from University at Buffalo's South Campus offering diverse variety of noodles and broths. Creamy tonkotsu, curry pork, Buffalo chicken, and green curry are among the more popular choices. Also recommended: okonomiyaki fries, topped with Japanese mayonnaise, barbecue-like okonomiyaki sauce, pickled sushi ginger, bonito flakes, and shredded nori seaweed.

Savage Wheat Project

savagewheat.com

Deluxe bakery goods without refined flour, sugar, or fat, mostly from heirloom grains is Emily Savage's jam. Her spelt sourdough bread, einkorn sourdough, and oat flour pancake-waffle mix helps people avoid reactions to modern wheat. Order through her website, by visiting one of the farm stores offering Savage Wheat, or via FreshFix.

Sahar Bakery

2784 Sheridan Drive, Tonawanda, 716-314-0116
Hours: 10 a.m.-8 p.m. Monday-Saturday. Closed Sunday.

Afghani couple in low-profile bakery offer barbari, the tray-sized dimpled loaves also known as Persian flatbread, in white and whole wheat, $5 for two loaves the size of skateboard decks. Plus roht, cardamom-scented semi-dry cake meant to be eaten with coffee or tea. Persian and Middle Eastern groceries like dried limes line the retail space, slightly larger than a minivan.

SEVENS

225 Louisiana Street, sevensbuffalo.com,
Instagram: @sevensbuffalo
Hours: 7 a.m.-4 p.m. Monday-Friday, 8 a.m.-5 p.m. Saturday,
8 a.m.-4 p.m. Sunday.

Vegan cafe and bakery turns heads with savory and
sweet confections. Vegan sausage rolls, cardamom
sticky buns, and seasonal delights are baked fresh
daily. Hoisin mushroom and harissa eggplant sandwiches make clear they're serious. Plus a full lineup of
matcha and coffee drinks tailed to match the vibe of
the month.

SAVOR

28 Old Falls St., 716-210-2580
Hours: during semester.

Each semester, value-seeking diners take note of the Niagara Falls Culinary Institute's academic schedule. That's because culinary students serve lunch and dinner under instruction at the school's first-floor restaurant. Currently, a steak dinner with appetizer and dessert goes for $35. Non-academic restaurants charge more like $60.

SCHWABL'S

789 Center Road, West Seneca, schwabls.com, 716-675-2333
Hours: 11:30 a.m.-7:30 p.m. Tuesday-Saturday.
Closed Sunday, Monday.

Destination beef-on-weck for those who love it rare,
Schwabl's cuts its beef to order. Enjoy the last German
family restaurant in the Buffalo area, with goulash
and German potato salad always on the menu – and
if you're lucky, today's soup is liver dumplings in beef
broth.

Shamus

98 West Ave., Lockport, shamuslockport.com,
716-433-9809
Hours: noon-8:30 p.m. Tuesday-Thursday, noon-9 p.m.
Friday, 3 p.m.-9 p.m. Saturday. Closed Sunday, Monday.

Generous bread basket, hand-cut onion rings, and reliable fish and chips bring diners back to this 35-year
veteran, still run by the Murphy family. To be sure,
many customers are there for the drinking to be had
at the copper-topped bar, but when it's time to take
the family out in Lockport, Shamus is one fine answer.

SHAWARMA HOUSE

824 E. Main St., Welland, Ont., shawarmahouse1.ca,
905-735-0777
Hours: 11 a.m.-9 p.m. Sunday-Wednesday,
11 a.m.-10 p.m. Thursday-Saturday.

The sort of Lebanese restaurant I wish Buffalo had
more of, with a pastry case, coffee bar, posters of Bei-
rut, and a bookshelf full of hookahs. Mixed shawarma
plate of chicken and beef, and lots of toum, Lebanese
garlic sauce, does not miss. Also recommended: kibbe,
deep-fried fritters that pack ground beef and pine nuts
in bulgur wheat and beef shell.

Shibam Mediterranean Restaurant

727 Kenmore Ave., 716-248-2288
Hours: 10 a.m.-10 p.m. Wednesday-Monday. Closed Tuesday.

Huge values for lamb lovers and others at quiet Yemeni family restaurant. Fresh bread, bubbling saltah and fasah stews, and ful medames are among its other attractions. As befitting Yemeni custom, sit-down customers can enjoy complimentary red tea and a cup of broth.

SIMPLY SOUL

829 Main St., Niagara Falls, 716-299-7105
Hours: 1 p.m.-9 p.m. Tuesday-Saturday, 1 p.m.-8 p.m. Sunday.
Closed Monday.

Classic soul food plates from a family operation hit all the right notes. Righteous oxtails with meat tender enough to tickle away from the bone, crispy well-seasoned catfish nuggets, definitive fried chicken, and cornbread from the cake side of the argument make it worth a visit.

SOFRA RESTAURANT AND BAKERY

38 Patrick Lane, Depew,
sofrarestaurantandbakery.com,
716-901-7200
Hours: noon-9 p.m. Tuesday-Sunday. Closed Monday.

Buffalo finally has a Turkish restaurant. Enjoy beyti kabab, grilled seasoned beef grilled in lavash dough. Other made-to-order bread-based dishes like lahmacun, pide, and karadeniz yagli, plus a full-scale dessert bakery counter have been drawing folks to Patrick Lane, just a mile from Buffalo-Niagara International Airport.

Sophia's

715 Military Road,
716-248-1235
Hours: 7 a.m.-3 p.m. Tuesday-Saturday, 7 a.m.-2 p.m. Sunday. Closed Monday.

My favorite old-school Buffalo diner, now in expanded digs, brings me back for chicken tender souvlaki breakfasts, with housemade bread. Dig blueberry pancakes, hot beef sandwiches with gravy, and the best avgolemono chicken-lemon-egg soup in town.

SOUTHERN BELLE DINER

3575 Walden Ave., Lancaster,
www.southernbellediner.com, 716-393-3033
Hours: 7 a.m.-3 p.m. daily

Texas diner classics like real chicken fried steak with country gravy, green chile cheese grits, fried okra, and huevos rancheros with queso bring faithfuls back to the table. Properly browned hash browns, lard in the beans, and cinnamon rolls add to the luster of a rare diner flavor in Western New York.

SOUTHERN JUNCTION

365 Connecticut Ave., southernjunction716.com
Hours: 4 p.m.-9 p.m. Monday, Thursday-Saturday,
10 a.m. -3 p.m. Sunday. Closed Tuesday, Wednesday.

Ryan Fernandez invented a cuisine that merges Texas
barbecue and Keralan Indian influences, getting
national recognition. Traditional barbecue joints start
with a line, where you wait to make your selections
from available meats and sides. It's worth the wait.

SPRESH INDIAN SUPERMARKET

3355 Sheridan Drive, Amherst, spresh.com, 716-836-0200
Hours: 10 a.m.-9 p.m. daily.

Well-stocked Indian and Bangladeshi grocery with fresh fruit, vegetables, and herbs, freezer section, and shelves of groceries. Plus a restaurant – Masala Memories – offering ready-to-eat samosas, pakoras, dosas, and more.

STRONG HEARTS BUFFALO

295 Niagara St., stronghearts716.com, 716-635-1777
Hours: Hours: 11 a.m.-8 p.m. Monday-Thursday, 11 a.m.-9 p.m. Friday, 10 a.m-9 p.m. Saturday, 10 a.m.-8 p.m. Sunday.

Vegan diner with uncanny animal-free menu started in Syracuse. Mac and cheese, milkshakes, cupcakes, Santa Fe chicken salads with ranch, burgers, fried chicken sandwiches, wings, and cheesesteaks, the whole gamut, all plant-based. Plus tasty enough to satisfy carnivores, a rare feat.

Suenos de Azucar Bakery

56 Niagara St., 716-533-8470
Hours: 8 a.m.-5 p.m. Tuesday-Friday.
Closed Saturday-Monday.

New Puerto Rican panaderia two blocks from Buffalo City Hall wows with guava pastelillos, mega queso rolls, and beef-and-plantain fried turnovers. Sandwiches like the Cubano and tripleta are big enough for a day's calories, stuffed with meat and salad fixings before being anointed with garlic oil.

THAT GREEK GUY BAKERY

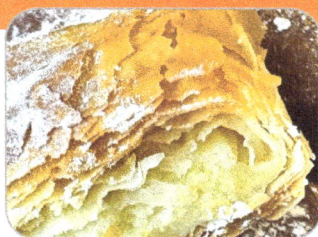

999 Broadway, Buffalo NY, greekguybakery.com,
716-200-9825
Hours: 7:30 a.m.-1 p.m. Tuesday, 11 a.m.-1:30 p.m.
Wednesday, 11 a.m.-2 p.m. Thursday, Friday,
10 a.m.-2 p.m. Saturday. Closed Sunday.

Michael Giokas and his son Alex offer pocket pita bread
that reminds people of Pete's Lebanese. Personally, I thrill
to the bougatsa, custard baked inside golden-brown
folded phyllo dusted with powdered sugar. Baklava, and
more are to be had, and That Greek Guy Bakery pita is
delivered to both Lexington Co-ops weekly.

Taqueria Los Mayas

3525 Genesee St., Cheektowaga, taqueria-los-mayas.co,
716-906-3730
Hours: 11 a.m.-8:30 p.m. Tuesday-Saturday.
Closed Sunday, Monday.

Best-in-town tacos start with housemade tortillas, and add carefully seared toppings. Then customers make it personal with a 25-choice toppings and salsa bar. Real cheese in the choriqueso, bacon and jalapenos in charro beans, and lard in refritos, helps it stand out from the Mexican crowd.

Thai House

5246 Transit Road, Depew, depewthaihouse.com,
716-601-7114
Hours: Hours: 11 a.m.-9 p.m. Monday-Saturday.
Closed Sunday.

Between the Thai, Burmese, Malaysian, and Japanese
dishes on the menu, everyone can find their own
favorite. Standouts include pork and mustard green
soup, Malaysian-style roast chicken, and Burmese
claypot biryani with cashews and fried garlic.

THIS LITTLE PIG

10651 Main St., Clarence, this-littlepigeats.com, 716-580-7872
Hours: 5 p.m.-9 p.m., Tuesday-Thursday, 5 p.m.-10 p.m. Friday, Saturday.
Closed Sunday, Monday.

There's lots of barbecue on Jeff Cooke Jr.'s menu, and a bevy of all-American desserts. But notions from the rest of the world, like a chicken-based version of Moroccan bisteeya, appear as specials. Standouts include piggy pipe bombs, smoked sausage-stuffed chiles , and shaved brussels sprouts salad with smoked peanuts

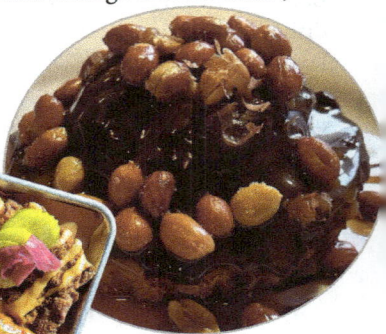

TIENDA MONTE ALBAN

507 E. Center St., Medina,
585-798-9767
4152 W. Main Street Road,
Batavia, 585-219-4081
Hours: 10 a.m.-8 p.m. daily.

Get a dozen types of dried chiles by the piece, spices, sauces, and cases of tortillas by heading to these Mexican groceries. In Medina, and one mile from the Batavia Thruway exit, lovers of Mexican cuisine can shop where the Mexicans do. Protip: Batavia tienda is in the same plaza as Taqueria Oaxaquena, which also earned a place in this guide.

TINY THAI

27 Chandler St. Suite 212B, tinythai.biz, 716-335-0474
Hours: 3 p.m.-9 p.m. Tuesday-Friday, 3 p.m.-8 p.m.
Friday, 1 p.m.-9 p.m. Saturday, Sunday.
Closed Monday.

Kae Baramee is a Thai native who grinds her own curry paste for coconut curries, one of the touches that make her takeout spot and truck a beacon for fans. Standouts include gai yang grilled sticky chicken, chicken-and-peanut-stuffed chor muang dumplings, shaped like blue flowers, and hat yai fried chicken.

TORTUGA

3189 Delaware Ave., Kenmore, tortugasandwich.com,
716-216-6003
Hours: 11 a.m.-6:30 p.m. Tuesday-Saturday.
Closed Sunday, Monday.

A Bolivian woman married a guy from Buffalo, which is how we got this rare outlet for South American flavors. Argentine, Colombian, Peruvian and Mexican dishes can be served as sandwiches, rice or grain boxes, salads, or loaded fries. Lomo saltado, the Peruvian steak and potato dish, shows up as the Chino, with Peruvian cheese sauce and chimichurri.

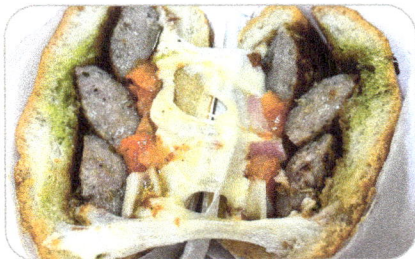

UKRAINIAN-AMERICAN CIVIC CENTER

205 Military Road, 716-877-7200
Hours: Friday, 5 p.m.-9 p.m.
Otherwise a membership social club.

Ukrainian cooking past pierogi is hard to come by in Buffalo. But Friday nights, the Ukrainian-American Civic Center is open to the public, so they can enjoy the cooking of Maria Hanypsiak, a Ukrainian grandmother who makes mushroom dumplings for the borscht, and dips her panfried fish in an eggy batter.

UNDERGROUNDS
COFFEE HOUSE

580 South Park Ave., undergroundscoffeebuffalo.com,
716-240-9923
Hours: 6 a.m.-2 p.m. Monday-Friday,
7:30 a.m.-3 p.m. Saturday, Sunday.

Former funeral home was transformed into a neighborhood caffeination center without losing its spooky charm. Get a bagel sandwich and a cup of coffee, think about joining the mug club's custom-designed lineup, and buy a pound of South-Buffalo-roasted coffee for your kitchen.

VINNIE'S MINIS

2789 Niagara St., Niagara Falls, 716-804-2184
Hours: 8 a.m.-5 p.m. Wednesday-Friday, 10 a.m-5 p.m.
Saturday. Closed Sunday-Tuesday.

Heat-and-eat pizzas in your supermarket freezer is
the main reason Vinnie's exists. But if you visit the Niagara Falls mother ship, you can dig into a variety of
pizzas, fresh bread, and monster sandwiches made on
that fresh bread. Worth a detour for culinary tourists.

Wasabi Amherst

100 Plaza Drive Suite C, Amherst, wasabi-buffalo.com,
716-689-5888
Hours: 11 a.m.-9 p.m. Monday-Thursday, 11 a.m.-10
p.m. Friday, Saturday. Closed Sunday.

One of Buffalo's best sushi options is a quiet room near
Hopkins and Klein in Amherst. Fresh fish handles with
respect, plus an excellent lineup of cooked dishes, like
hamachi kama, seared yellowtail collar, the bone-in
pork chop of the sea. Fried noodles, salmon skin salad,
and custardy fried age tofu are some of my favorites.

WAXLIGHT
BAR A VIN

27 Chandler St., waxlightbaravin.com
Hours: 5 p.m.-10 p.m. Wednesday, Thursday, 5 p.m.-11 p.m.
Friday, Saturday. Closed Sunday-Tuesday.

Creative restaurant with first-class service and award-winning eats and drinks. Craft in every plate, from two-bite appetizers like anchovy toast with horseradish vinaigrette, to big kahunas like dry-aged beef coulotte "bourguignon," cremini mushroom, beef bacon, with pommes dauphine. Expert drinks staff will help you find a new favorite.

WAYLAND BREWING COMPANY

3740 N. Buffalo St., Orchard Park, 716-755-2509
Hours: 4 p.m.-9 p.m. Monday, Wednesday, Thursday, 11:30
a.m.-9 p.m. Friday, 11 a.m.-9 p.m. Saturday,
11 a.m.-7 p.m. Sunday. Closed Tuesday.

The rare brewpub not poured into rehabbed industrial
space happens to be from the Grange folks. In clem-
ent weather bocce courts, picnic tables and firepits
help people congregate outside. Inside the light-
graced space serves from 17 taps, including a guest
cider, and a menu that includes Detroit-style pizza,
Nashville chicken sandwiches, and vegan smoked
cashew dip with guajillo salsa.

WEST ROSE

23 Washington St., Ellicottville, westrose.restaurant,
716-699-9113
Hours: 4:30 p.m.-9:30 p.m. Wednesday-Saturday,
10:30 a.m.-2 p.m. brunch, 4 p.m.-8 p.m. Sunday.
Closed Monday, Tuesday.

Anthony Petrilli's menu turns local bounty into estimable plates, from simple to profound. Housemade
focaccia, whipped ricotta and Calabrian chile, to steak
frites and smoked chicken over braised kale and black
pepper and pecorino polenta Also note the Wayland
Brewing Company popup upstairs, 4:30 p.m.-10 p.m.
Friday, Saturday.

WIECHEC'S LOUNGE

1748 Clinton St., facebook.com/Wiechecs, 716-823-2828
Hours: 11 a.m.-10 p.m. Monday-Thursday, 11 a.m.-11
p.m. Friday, Saturday. Closed Sunday.

Old-school Buffalo tavern with sprawling menu
besides its standing-room-only fish fry. Sure, there's
burgers, wings, and salads. There's also a huge
beer-battered chicken sandwich, liverwurst on rye,
Vernor's highballs, and a devastatingly effective taco
soup numbered amongst its stand-up satisfactions.

WINFIELD'S PUB

1213 Ridge Road, Lackawanna, winfieldspub.com,
716-821-0700
Hours: 4 p.m.-9 p.m. Monday, Wednesday, Thursday,
4 p.m.-9:30 p.m. Friday, Saturday.
Closed Sunday, Tuesday.

Master chef Tab Daulton has the best tavern menu in
town. My favorite poutine, house-cut fries with duck
gravy and cheese curds or chevre. Enjoy pork fran-
caise, fish tacos, pork belly burnt ends, and creamy
fish fry soup with beer batter crunchies for lent, and
Kiki's warm potato salad, with Velveeta, bacon, and
green olives.

Wok & Roll

5467 Sheridan Dr, Amherst, thewokandroll.com,
716-631-8880
Hours: 11 a.m.-9 p.m. Monday-Saturday.
Closed Sunday.

Solid American Chinese menu with a strong sideline
in Cantonese specialties, including a notable assortment of dumplings and other dim sum dishes. Its
"juicy buns" aren't soup dumplings, the Shanghaiese
xiao long bao, but they're close enough to take the
edge off.

Woo Chon
Korea House

402 Evans St., Amherst, woochonkoreahouse.com,
716-626-5980
Hours: 11:30 a.m.-9 p.m. Sunday, Wednesday, Thursday,
11:30 a.m.-9:30 p.m. Friday, Saturday.

Best-in-show Korean restaurant holds area's only
barbecue tables, inset with gas grill so diners can cook
their own barbecue. The array of banchan, side dishes,
rivals Koreatown, and the japchae, peppery stir-fried
sweet potato noodles, hits the mark.

Yalley's
African Restaurant

290 Kenmore Ave., yalleys.com, 716-322-1012
Hours: 11 a.m.-9 p.m. Sunday, Monday-Friday,
11 a.m.-midnight Saturday.

Ghanaian place that might inspire hankerings for African chow after your first visit. Here I'd try the fufu and peanut soup, jollof rice, and "red-red," black eyed peas simmered in palm oil. Buffalo and Ghana cuisine both appreciate fried poultry odds-and-ends: one Ghanaian specialty served here is deep-fried marinated turkey butts.

Yankee BBQ

4572 Clark St., Hamburg, yankeebbq716.com,
716-768-4991
Hours: noon-10:30 p.m. Wednesday-Friday,
10 a.m.-11 p.m. Saturday, 10 a.m.-7 p.m. Sunday.

Known for dinosaur-sized beef ribs, loganberry pork belly burnt ends, and smoked scalloped potatoes in Blasdell, the operation moved to a roomier spot in Hamburg with a full bar. Smoked beef cheek ramen, smoked fish fries, smoked-and-fried wings, and more delicious ideas have joined the menu.

YEMEN STAR

754 Sycamore St., yemenstarbuffalo.com, 716-381-8002
Hours: 9 a.m.-10 p.m. Monday-Saturday,
11 a.m.-10 p.m. Sunday.

You may hear only Arabic when you walk into this
Yemeni spot, but ordering in English was no problem.
Ful medames arrives with a waft of garlicky steam, in
a bubbling cauldron. With fresh bread, it can satisfy by
itself. But lamb haneeth, grilled chicken, and saltah and
fahsah stews also beckon.

ZAMBISTRO

408 Main St., Medina, zambis-
tro.com, 585-798-2433
Hours: 11 a.m.-9 p.m. Mon-
day-Thursday, 11 a.m.-10 p.m.
Friday, Saturday.
Closed Sunday.

Twenty years in, Michael Zambito's place has grown into Orleans County's best splurge-night destination. Adding a second-story deck and first-floor dining space has given Michael Zambito's place to show off its diverse modern American cuisine. Don't miss Nana's spinach bread.

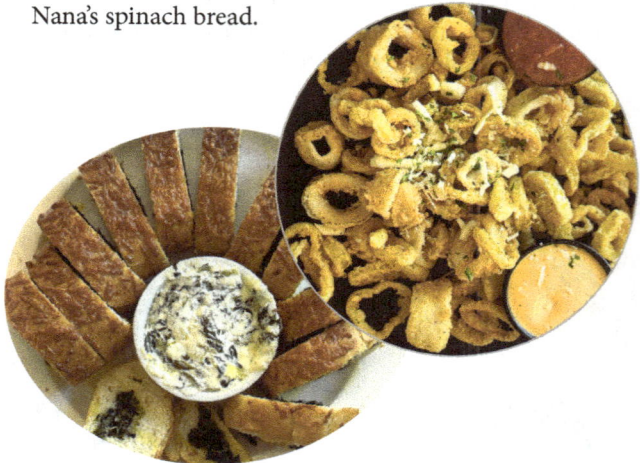

ZERESHK

704 Maple Road, Amherst,
zereshkny.com, 716-458-0081
Hours: 1 p.m.-9 p.m. daily.

New Persian restaurant offering made-to-order kebabs like the classic koobideh and stews like ghormeh sabzi, lamb with greens, kidney beans and tangy dried lime. Opened August 2025 by a couple who met down the road at UB's Amherst campus, it's not fast food, but worth the wait.

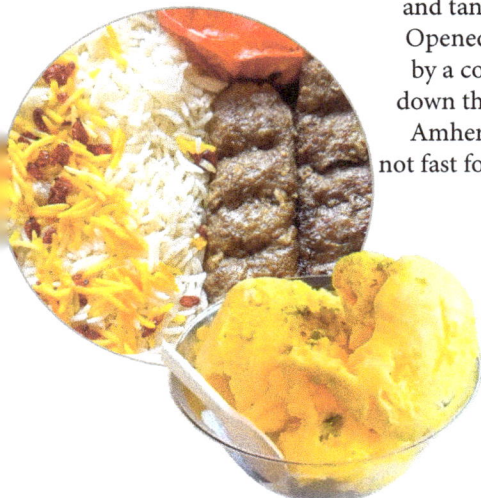

Photo Credits

While many photos in this guide were taken by the author, the following are credited to other sources:

Amabel: James Pici

Photos used by permission: Bailey Seafood, Bistro 93 Bloom & Rose, Bocce on Bailey, Coco Bar & Bistro, D'Alfonso's Italian Imports, Forno Napoli, Gondola Macaroni Products, Kith & Kin Bakeshop & Bistro, Kuni's. Lexington Co-op, Lovejoy Pizza, Picasso's Pizza, Raha Coffee House, Remedy House, Sevens, Undergrounds Coffee House.